SCOTNOTES
Number 27

Anne Donovan's

Buddha Da

Christopher Nicol

Association for Scottish Literary Studies 2010

Published by
Association for Scottish Literary Studies
Department of Scottish Literature
7 University Gardens
University of Glasgow
Glasgow G12 8QH
www.asls.org.uk

ASLS is a registered charity no. SC006535

First published 2010

© Christopher Nicol

All rights reserved. No part of this book may be reproduced, stored in a retrieval system, or transmitted in any form or means, electronic, mechanical, photocopying, recording or otherwise, without the prior permission of the Association for Scottish Literary Studies.

A CIP catalogue for this title
is available from the British Library

ISBN 978-1-906841-00-3

The Association for Scottish Literary Studies acknowledges the support of Creative Scotland towards the publication of this book.

Printed by Bell and Bain Ltd., Glasgow

CONTENTS

		Page
1.	Anne Donovan and her Work	1
2.	Approaching *Buddha Da*	4
	Introduction	4
	The language of the novel	5
	The setting of the novel	7
	Narrative structure	9
3.	Interpretative Summary	11
	A crisis in the making (pp.1–82)	11
	'Ah'm on a journey and ah don't know where ah'm gaun' (pp.83–151)	19
	The fragmenting family (pp.153–205)	30
	'You think that a funeral's the end but really it's the beginnin' (pp.205–330)	39
4.	**Characters**	**52**
	Jimmy	52
	Anne Marie	53
	Liz	54
5.	**Themes**	**58**
	The difficulties of family communication	58
	Negotiating change	61
6.	**Buddhism in *Buddha Da***	**65**
7.	**Further Reading: *Being Emily***	**69**
	Summary	69
	The Brontë connection	71
	The role of creativity	73
	The spiritual dimension	73
	The danger of assumptions	74
8.	**Selected Bibliography**	**76**

SCOTNOTES

Study guides to major Scottish writers and literary texts

Produced by the Education Committee
of the Association for Scottish Literary Studies

Series Editors
Lorna Borrowman Smith
Ronald Renton

Editorial Board
Ronald Renton, St Aloysius' College, Glasgow
(Convener, Education Committee, ASLS)
Jim Alison, HMI (retired)
Professor John Corbett, University of Glasgow
Dr Morna Fleming, Liberton High School
Professor Douglas Gifford, University of Glasgow
John Hodgart, Garnock Academy
Alan MacGillivray, Past President of ASLS
Catrina McGillivray, Newbattle Abbey College
Dr David Manderson, University of the West of Scotland
Dr Christopher Nicol, Galashiels Academy
Lorna Ramsay, Fairlie, Ayrshire
Professor Alan Riach, University of Glasgow
Dr Christine Robinson, Scottish Language Dictionaries
Dr Kenneth Simpson, University of Strathclyde
Lorna Borrowman Smith, formerly Wallace High School
Ailsa Stratton, Boroughmuir High School

THE ASSOCIATION FOR SCOTTISH LITERARY STUDIES aims to promote the study, teaching and writing of Scottish literature, and to further the study of the languages of Scotland.

To these ends, the ASLS publishes works of Scottish literature; literary criticism and in-depth reviews of Scottish books in *Scottish Literary Review*; short articles, features and news in *ScotLit*; and scholarly studies of language in *Scottish Language*. It also publishes *New Writing Scotland*, an annual anthology of new poetry, drama and short fiction, in Scots, English and Gaelic. ASLS has also prepared a range of teaching materials covering Scottish language and literature for use in schools.

All the above publications are available as a single 'package', in return for an annual subscription. Enquiries should be sent to:

>ASLS
>Department of Scottish Literature
>7 University Gardens
>University of Glasgow
>Glasgow G12 8QH
>
>Tel/fax +44 (0)141 330 5309
>e-mail **office@asls.org.uk**
>or visit our website at **www.asls.org.uk**

All references are to the Canongate paperback editions of Anne Donovan's work.

Generous assistance in the writing of this Scotnote has been received from Anne Donovan; Barbara Wills; Dr David Moses, Ampleforth College; Dr Jeremy Scott, University of Kent; Dr Margery Palmer McCulloch, University of Glasgow.

1. ANNE DONOVAN AND HER WORK

Originally from Coatbridge, Anne Donovan studied English and Philosophy at Glasgow University then became an English teacher. She continued in this role in various secondary schools until 2003 when, after the publication of her first novel, she made the transition to full-time writing.

Like many graduates in English, Anne Donovan found the process of studying the classics of English literature somewhat inhibiting to her own writing at first, discovering like many writers that analysing the work of the great names of the past can undermine self-confidence. She continued, nevertheless, in this post-university period, to write short stories sporadically, whenever her teaching duties permitted. A number of these later found their way into *Hieroglyphics and Other Stories* (2001), the first collection of her works to be published.

A breakthrough for her writing had come when she attended an Arvon Foundation writing course at Moniack Mhor in the Scottish Highlands in 1995, tutored by the novelist A.L. Kennedy and the poet Bill Herbert. This was the first time she had really shown her work to anyone of the calibre of Kennedy and Herbert, both of whom she found encouraging in their comments. It was here that she began to feel what she calls 'a huge internal shift in my consciousness'[1] in that exposure to critical analysis and encouragement of this kind made her feel writing was a wholly 'normal' activity and that she had a role to play in the writing community.

In the period before embarking on the Arvon course, she had written most of 'Hieroglyphics', the short story which later gave its name to the *Hieroglyphics and Other Stories* collection. This was a significant moment in her writing career since it was her first short story in the Scots vernacular, with which her work has come to be closely associated. Having most of this story to hand, she decided that it would be one of the pieces she showed to Bill Herbert, an acknowledged expert in writing in Scots. His positive reaction led to the final section of that particular short story being completed at Arvon.

This new-found confidence saw Anne Donovan in the late 1990s continuing to work on short stories which were later published in *Hieroglyphics and Other Stories*. One of these, 'All that Glisters', won the Macallan/Scotland on Sunday Prize in 1997, further boosting Donovan's belief in herself and bringing her work to the attention of an increasingly interested public.

Underlining her commitment to writing was her decision to embark on the MLitt course in Creative Writing run by the Universities of Glasgow and Strathclyde, a bold step given her existing workload from her teaching, to say nothing of the growing demands of her own writing. This augured well for the future, since on the day Anne Donovan began this course in 1999, she discovered that her short story 'Millennium Babe' had won the Canongate Prize for New Writing and was to be published in 2000 in the prizewinners anthology, *Scotland Into The New Era*. Thus began a hugely fertile period in her development. During these study years, she was tutored by Margaret Elphinstone and Willy Maley, both of whom she found highly constructive critics of her work. Of this period she comments:

> It is always difficult to understand where influence is coming from. I think I already had a fairly clear idea (maybe too clear!) of what I was doing at that time. But writers such as Grassic Gibbon, Tom Leonard, Liz Lochhead and Alan Spence among others were influential. I also think that, as well as the tutors, the other students were a great support. We were all working to improve our writing and there were folk around who wanted to talk about, read and discuss it.[2]

Midway through her part-time course, the Scottish Arts Council awarded Anne Donovan a bursary in 2000 which allowed her to cut down on her teaching commitments and concentrate more on writing.

This intervention was timely. Around this same time the Canongate publishing house, which had already acknowledged her talent with their earlier award, stepped back into her life. Jamie Byng, the owner of Canongate, had been a judge both in the Macallan award and in his own Canongate Prize. Anne Donovan comments:

> At the awards ceremony for the Canongate award Jamie spoke to me, saying he'd only ever judged two competitions and I'd won both, so perhaps I should send him work! By then I had written quite a few stories and was starting what would become *Buddha Da*. I got a contract for *Hieroglyphics*, to be followed by *Buddha Da* when it was finished. Canongate were quite visionary in publishing short stories.[3]

Her collection *Hieroglyphics and Other Stories* was published in 2001 to considerable acclaim. In 2003 the publication by Canongate of her first novel *Buddha Da* was followed soon after by its inclusion on the shortlist of potential winners of the prestigious Orange Prize for Fiction. Shortly afterwards *Buddha Da* was nominated for the Whitbread First Novel Award, sealing Anne Donovan's place as one of the leading writers of her generation. In 2004 *Buddha Da* was shortlisted for the Scottish Art Council's 'Book of the Year' and won the Prince Maurice Award in Mauritius. The same year saw Donovan adapting the short story 'Hieroglyphics' into a one-act play which was staged at Oran Mor in Glasgow and later published in an ASLS anthology, *Plays for Schools*. A second novel, *Being Emily*, followed in 2008 (see Chapter 7, **Further Reading**).

Notes
1. E-mail to *Scotnote* author, 8 December 2008.
2. Ibid.
3. Ibid.

2. APPROACHING *BUDDHA DA*

Introduction

Published in 2003, *Buddha Da* follows the fortunes of Jimmy McKenna and his family from the early summer of 1999 to the summer of 2000. It began life as a short story in which Anne Marie McKenna recounts how her father became involved in Buddhism and set off to Carmunnock to find a baby that was reputed to be a reincarnation of a Buddhist leader.

Reflecting on the various ways the family of this Glasgow house-painter might be affected by his preoccupation with Buddhism, Anne Donovan very quickly realised that the idea had richer possibilities than had at first been apparent. Accordingly, she revised her short story material into novel form. After this preliminary Carmunnock episode, the central action of the novel could be said to start where it finally reaches its resolution, at the seaside holiday cottage which the McKennas and Liz's mother take annually. This cyclical format underlines the fact that Jimmy, Liz and Anne Marie arrive at the place from where they started with a clearer idea of who they are and what they value in each other. The summer of 1999 is overshadowed by the failing health of Liz's mother; the summer of 2000 anticipates the arrival of Liz's baby. In between, the reader encounters events set in motion by Jimmy's preoccupation with Buddhism which, far from bringing him the peace which meditation promised, succeeds in wreaking havoc with the lives of the entire family.

Jimmy McKenna is a successful, self-employed painter and decorator who owns his own property; his wife, Liz, holds down a responsible job in a lawyer's office; their daughter Anne Marie is musically talented and doing well at school. The McKennas exist in a strong network of social relationships, as is evident at the funeral of Liz's mother, where, in addition to close family members, a wide cross-section of people from Maryhill and beyond feels an obligation to attend. On the perimeters of the novel, Jimmy's brother and his wife play small but significant roles in the lives of Jimmy and Liz. The society depicted is far from broken and, while family ties may become badly strained at times, they are never entirely severed.

In addition to being socially cohesive, the society described here is also culturally diverse, with Catholic, Buddhist, Sikh and Tibetan elements existing side-by-side in seeming communal harmony. Such disturbances which are caused by Buddhism are rather those occasioned by Jimmy's muddled interpretation of it rather than by any ideological conflict. Indeed, we see that it is his daughter's successful ability to interact with and absorb non-native influences which brings her a great sense of self-fulfilment. She learns to integrate her traditional Catholic music-making with novel Tibetan input in a way that brings her a sense of achievement and, indeed, acclaim. This successful integration of tradition and change also provides the final pages of the novel with a possible model for family reconciliation. To date the McKennas have been a traditional Catholic family; now, as they await the birth of Liz's love-child, they will have to extend and change the traditional definition of family if their lives are to be complete. Will they succeed? Subtly, Donovan leaves the question open.

The language of the novel

As the nationalist wave took hold in Scotland during the latter decades of the twentieth century, so, too, did the interest of Scottish writers in demotic Scots (the dialects of everyday speech in Scotland) which Donovan uses here. In some ways there was nothing new in this; Scottish writing through the centuries had been rich in demotic voices, but usually to introduce local colour into dialogue. With writers such as James Kelman, Irvine Welsh, Alan Warner and Jeff Torrington, however, Scots in the latter years of the twentieth century was elevated to take over as the principal narrative language of many novels and short stories.

For some writers such as Kelman, the interest was sociopolitical: his aim was to liberate his writing from what he saw as the colonising tyranny of Standard English, thus giving a literary language to working-class Scots. Anne Donovan also makes claims for the legitimacy of Scots (or more particularly here, Glaswegian) as a literary language but her intention seems apolitical, more a desire to celebrate the lyrical richness of the daily language of Jimmy, Liz and Anne

Marie. One commentator has spoken of 'the sheer sensual pleasure that we get from the language ... and the exhilarating depth of expression it allows us.'[1] Another suggests her writing 'portrays Scots as the natural language of feeling and emotion.'[2] Donovan, too, sees its usefulness for getting in touch with the sentiments of her characters: 'It's more a direct line to the heart, you get closer.'[3] Donovan had hoped originally to get even closer by differentiating the three family voices: 'I thought at first maybe I'll make the mum less broad, but I decided to keep them the same.'[4] (Alert readers, however, may notice that Liz, perhaps due to her job in a lawyer's office, has stretches of speech which owe much to Standard English.)

The use of Scots demotic has in no way limited the novel's appeal for readers beyond the Scottish border. Reviewing it, London-based writer Patrick Gale commented: 'I've always found Scots more comprehensible to the ear than the eye, so it's a credit to Donovan's narrative skill that after ten pages I was only noticing differences in language when unfamiliar pleasures cropped up.'[5] Articulated by Donovan, the demotic voice has the linguistic flexibility to catch convincingly the novel's switches of mood. These range from the dry humour of:

> Mammy and me had just got back fae the Co-op when the lamas arrived at the door. (p.6)

to the crispness of Liz's exasperation with Jimmy when he announces his need for celibacy in aid of clarity:

> 'If ah have tae wait tae you get mair clarity afore we have it aff ah'll be deid.' (p.108)

to the poetic tenderness of Jimmy as he watches the pregnant Liz on the beach:

> Ah looked at her, sittin on the sand, the breeze blowin strands of her hair in front of her eyes [...] And the beach stretched oot behind her tae a blue sea and a blue sky dotted wi clouds. It was like every year's holiday photie; different

hairstyles, different claes, but the same auld sea, same sky, same Liz. (p.325)

As Donovan herself remarks: 'The more particular you make something, the more grounded it is, the more it can resonate.'[6] The firm grounding of her characters in their own speech world does indeed resonate powerfully, and far afield, too. In 2004 *Buddha Da* won the Prince Maurice Award in Mauritius, proving that demotic Scots can transcend national barriers to enjoy international acclaim.

The setting of the novel
Writers from James Hogg to Ian Rankin, when writing about the nation's capital, have tended to insist on the dualism of Edinburgh: the respectable face hiding a darker heart. The depiction of Glasgow in fiction, however, is less fixated on a dual identity. Like Paris and New York, it enjoys a more multifaceted portrayal in literature. Moira Burgess's description of it as 'Kaleidoscope City'[7] is wholly apt. For some writers like Alan Spence in *The Magic Flute* or Hugh Munro in *The Clydesiders* it is a city of sectarianism and violence. Others such as George Blake in *The Shipbuilders* see it as a more humane, if economically deprived, environment. In Dot Allan's *Hunger March* we see a city of poverty and yet a certain solidarity. For Louise Welsh in *The Cutting Room* it is a city of vice-ridden materialism where love 'can be folded and put in your pocket'.

Anne Donovan's Glasgow is a gentler one than is sometimes found in Glasgow-centred fiction. Poverty, violence, sectarianism, politics and consumerism play no part in it at all. The difficulties characters encounter are the result of family tensions rather than social friction. Catholic, Buddhist, Sikh and Tibetan elements coexist without the raising of an authorial eyebrow, presenting a postcolonial, cosmopolitan backdrop in which national and ideological differences seem ultimately to enrich rather than encroach on each other. Nearer home, within the McKenna household, however, this successful blending of cultures is, initially, far from being the case, but the figure of Anne Marie grows to reflect the cultural and ideological synthesis that is embodied in Donovan's view of twenty-first century Glasgow.

Although resolutely Glaswegian in her dialect and Catholic in her religion, Anne Marie nevertheless finds comfort for much of the novel in the company of her Sikh friend, Nisha, whose disc-jockey brother, Gurpreet, specialises in 'sampling', that is to say, mixing Indian, hiphop and European music to create a harmonious new blend of influences in which national characteristics are effaced to create a new stateless synthesis. This is the basis for Anne Marie's successful blending of Catholic and Buddhist traditions in her acclaimed CD. She is also open to a popular international culture which effortlessly embraces heterogeneous items such as the films *Titanic*, *Ratcatcher*, television programmes such as *Who Wants to be a Millionaire?* and *EastEnders*, the music of Andrew Lloyd Webber and Madonna. The recurring references to Madonna, Anne Marie's idol, are not a coincidence: she is an artist who is constantly alert to new influences, enjoying a long career through successfully reinventing herself. Like Anne Marie, she thrives on the challenge of change.

This is a Glasgow in which the cultural, national and religious frontiers are becoming increasingly blurred through a combination of free international movement, cross-cultural exchanges and the levelling dominance of global popular culture, a Glasgow of the young and, Donovan seems to hint, the Glasgow of the future.

So already embedded is this cultural synthesis among the young that when Anne Marie's class visits the Buddhist centre (pp.258–9) real confusion arises when Kevin attempts to define fellow-pupil Khalil as being from India. The futility of the old labels is made clear:

> 'That's where you come fae in't it, Khalil?' says Kevin.
> 'Don't be daft, he comes fae Pakistan.'
> 'Ah do not,' says Khalil. 'Ah come fae Govan.'

It must be remembered, however, that *Buddha Da* foregrounds the life of the McKennas, their friends and family more than the life of Glasgow as a whole. Nevertheless, the city backdrop against which the action unrolls is one where sectarian divides and social fragmentation seem increasingly distant as the new millennium dawns.

Narrative structure
The novel advances by means of Jimmy, Liz and Anne Marie each taking turns to narrate concurrent events. This turn-taking allows the reader to enter into the mindset and experience of each of these likeable but often unhappy family members, a privilege the McKennas often deny to each other as they struggle to understand the bewildering events which overtake them. This narrative approach is much more than a stylistic device. It goes to the heart of one of the novel's central ideas: we tend to see things very much from our own point of view, not realising how they may affect those closest to us.

Anne Marie both opens and closes the novel, although Jimmy's early exposition of his first encounter with Buddhism occupies the greatest single narrative episode. Liz, however, is the family member to whom much of the narrative is entrusted – 139 pages to Jimmy's 88 and Anne Marie's 73. Such narrative weighting in Liz's favour is perhaps no surprise, given that she is the McKenna who reflects most on the events which rock this once stable household.

Within this tripartite narrative pattern the novel may be seen to fall into four main episodes:

- the first ending with the birthday party to celebrate Jimmy's brother's fortieth birthday;
- the second concludes with Jimmy leaving home after the millennium celebrations;
- the third ends with the funeral of Liz's mother;
- the final section deals with what happens to Liz in the aftermath of Jimmy's departure and her mother's death.

Notes
1. Rosemary Goring: 'She's talking our language now', *The Herald*, 4 January 2003

2. Jeremy Scott, 'Talking Back at the Centre: Demotic Language in Contemporary Scottish Fiction', *Literature Compass* 2 20C 148, (1–26)
3. Anne Donovan, in Goring article above
4. Anne Donovan, in Goring article above
5. Patrick Gale, 'A Pint of Heavy and a Glass of Moselle', *Daily Telegraph*, 8 March 2003
6. Anne Donovan, in Goring article above
7. Moira Burgess, *Imagine a City: Glasgow in Literature*, Argyll Press, 1998, p.181

3. INTERPRETATIVE SUMMARY

A crisis in the making (pp.1–82)
When Jimmy sets off on his fruitless trip to Carmunnock in the company of the Tibetan lamas to find the reincarnation of an important lama, he finds great difficulty in finding the place and, once there, discovers he has had a wasted journey: the child turns out to be a girl. Comic though this episode deliberately is, it prefigures in miniature much of what will happen to Jimmy, in a more serious way, in the course of the novel as a whole: on his journey of self-discovery he will take several wrong turnings. This latter journey, like the trip to Carmunnock, will also end with a baby – but the baby in both cases turns out to be not quite the one that might have been anticipated.

Jimmy McKenna, his daughter Anne Marie points out, is a thorough-going extrovert with a wild and unpredictable streak:

> Ma da's a nutter. Radio rental. He'd dae anything for a laugh so he wid; went doon the shops wi a perra knickers on his heid, tellt the wifie next door we'd won the lottery and were flittin tae Barbados [...] (p.1)

He is well-known for taking up projects and dropping them:

> Wanst it wis building a gairden shed, anither time it wis strippin an auld sideboard that came fae ma granny's. And of course he'd start it then get fed up and no finish. It drives ma ma roon the bend. (p.3)

His interest in Buddhism appears initially to his wife and daughter as no different from any of his other passing fads. But for Jimmy his trip to the Buddhist centre is different:

> They were dead nice, dead ordinary, gied me a cuppa tea, showed me the meditation room, and, ach, it wis the atmosphere, hen. Ah cannae explain it, but it wis just dead calm. (p.2)

Explaining his new preoccupation will indeed be a problem for Jimmy throughout the novel. Quizzed by Anne Marie, he seems rather vague about his new-found interest in Buddhism:

> 'Ah'm no sure how tae stert. It's difficult tae explain.'
> 'Aye, but, whit d'you dae?'
> 'Well you sit doon quiet and you try tae empty yer mind, well no exactly empty, mair quiet it doon so aw the thoughts that go fleein aboot in yer heid kinda slow doon and don't annoy ye.'
> 'Why?'
> 'Ah'm no very sure masel, hen.' (p.4)

He is equally vague when questioned about his prayer beads:

> 'Who dae you pray tae?'
> There was a funny look on his face.
> 'Look hen, this isnae easy, ah'm no really sure masel whit's happenin, ach …' (p.5)

Although far from sure what his new interest is all about, there is no doubting Jimmy's dedication to it. Equally clear is the strength of his relationship with Liz. Although she will be seen to be increasingly hostile and bewildered by Jimmy's preoccupation with Buddhism, the bond between them is strong – as is seen when the family is on holiday at their seaside cottage. She recounts how

> Jimmy grabbed me, liftin me high oot the water then doon and ah caught ma breath for a minute and shut ma eyes, feelin the cauld water and the heat aff the sun and the nearness of him all at once. He jumped me again, pushin me high in the air then letting me doon again, and the two of us stood there, just lookin at each other. Him silhouetted against the sun, his face dark and his hair glintin bright and he was laughin. (p.20)

Liz on holiday, however, is a woman with much on her mind: her mother's failing health (p.17), Jimmy's uncharacteristic desire to be on his own to meditate (p.23) and her own unspoken desire to have another child (pp.23–24). Just like the holiday jigsaw she muses over, Liz's life is incomplete but she seems incapable of talking to Jimmy about this. Of her worry about his new solitariness she remarks:

> Ah knew we should talk but ah kept puttin it aff. (p.23)

But this conversation will never take place.

Once home, Jimmy seeks to advance his meditation skills at a Buddhist retreat. The visit is not an unmitigated success. His bantering cheeriness cannot disguise his difficulties with getting to grips with Buddhism. He cannot concentrate on his meditation for remembering how he and Liz had parted:

> Ah'd went tae kiss her but she turnt her face away and that wis whit kept comin back tae me as ah tried tae focus on ma breathin. (p.29)

He feels definitely 'ooty place' (p.26); he takes a dislike to Vishana who runs the weekend, feeling there is 'sumpn smarmy aboot him ah didnae like' (p.32); he feels lost when the discussion turns to reincarnation which was 'sumpn ah couldnae get ma heid roond' (p.34). And to crown his problems, he gashes his hand quite seriously peeling carrots, 'which is why ah'm staundin here lookin like a scene fae *Reservoir Dogs*' (p.36). Light though Donovan's touch is here, there is no doubting that Jimmy is struggling hard to come to terms with Buddhism. Much of what is discussed passes over his head, including a comment lightly made by a fellow member of the retreat:

> 'Truly being in the present encompasses both the past and the future. You have to hold them all together as one.' (p.35)

As we shall see in Jimmy's behaviour after his brother's fortieth birthday party, failure to understand this tenet of Buddhism will be at the root of much of his later unhappiness, seeking as he later does to divorce himself artificially from elements in his past which shame him.

Finally, Jimmy admits defeat:

> Ah'd gied up on the meditation, couldnae concentrate again. Ah wis tired and everythin that had happened ower the weekend so far wis churnin away inside me; the new folk, the stuff ah couldnae unnerstaund, Vishana and they fuckin carrots, and ah felt weary in ma bones. (p.39)

The weekend, however, is not without its compensations. He has taken great delight in the autumn beauty of the trees (p.31) and in just sitting listening to the raindrops falling on the glass roof of the prayer room:

> And it wis like the rain wis alive, know, and everythin in the prayer room seemed tae disappear, couldnae hear anybuddy or see anythin; it wis just me and the rain. (p.39)

The irony here is that Jimmy has put himself to great trouble to understand the mysteries of eastern meditation and has failed miserably so far; yet his own innate sensitivity to beauty around him brings him the peace that eludes him in Buddhist meditation. This irony seems to escape him entirely, but then Jimmy is someone who lives and feels for the moment rather than someone who reflects over the implications of his experiences, as the novel gradually reveals.

He returns home to a frosty welcome from Liz (p.39) and, while he quietly seethes inwardly at what he sees as Liz's condescending attitude to his interest in Buddhism (p.42), he, like Liz, never gets round to discussing the matter openly, thus sowing the seeds for later unhappiness. Temporarily, they get over this episode by the strength of their physical attraction for each other (pp.44–45) but neither takes advantage of this outbreak of peace to discuss the deep underlying divisions that threaten them, preferring instead to discuss the amusing eccentricities of Jimmy's clients (pp.45–46).

Jimmy's Buddhist education takes a step forward when Barbara Mellis, a researcher he had met on retreat, invites him to decorate part of her Edinburgh flat. Once Jimmy determines she has no romantic interest in him, the pair of them bond well. The scenes in Barbara's flat reveal Jimmy in his professional role for the first time. While he may struggle with Buddhism, there is no doubting his integrity, knowledge and competence in his trade. He explains to Barbara how, exasperated by working for an unprincipled employer, he and his brother, John, took matters into their own hands:

> 'So me and John decided tae set up on wer ain, dae things properly.'
> 'I like that, it shows you've got integrity.'
> 'Well who wants tae dae folk? Fair's fair – you may as well dae it right. And the thing is, it pays in the long run.'
> (p.57)

Here at least, Jimmy is properly in tune with Buddhism. As Barbara comments:

> 'Right livelihood. Very Buddhist.'

Jimmy finds great satisfaction and peace in his work:

> There was a lot of footery stuff – cornice she wanted picked oot in different colours – and ah really like daein them [...] ah spent maisty the time quiet, just paintin. It was dead peaceful in the hoose and thon big statue of the Buddha; well, it was like she said, it had a calming presence. When she came in the room ah near fell aff the ladder, ah'd forgotten there was embdy else there.
> 'Christ, ah goat a fright – ah was in another world there.'
> (pp.54–55)

While this may not be the peace of meditation, there is no questioning the serenity work brings him, a serenity akin to the peace he enjoyed listening to the rain on retreat. While

Jimmy doggedly pursues Buddhist meditation in search of peace, he seems totally unaware that his appreciation of nature and his enjoyment of his work are also capable of transporting him to 'another world' which also offers that elusive peace.

Barbara casually drops into conversation a crucially important idea whose full significance escapes Jimmy for much of the novel:

> 'Most people think Buddhism's about meditating, but it's really about how you live your whole life. Part of it is the idea that you make your living in a good way, not a harmful or dishonest one.'
>
> 'So all this time ah've been a Buddhist while ah'm paintin. Ah could have saved masel all that hassle meditatin.'
>
> 'I think maybe that's true – I don't mean that you shouldn't meditate, but … I don't know how to put it; it's as if we're always trying to get there, reach something, and that isn't it. It's being fully aware in the day to day that's important, being completely engaged in what we're doing. And maybe for you, it's the painting. When you're doing your job, you're fully present.' (p.57)

While Jimmy may be 'fully aware in the day to day' in his professional life, as we have just seen, this ideal as yet escapes him in his family life, oblivious as he is to the hurt and bewilderment he is causing his wife and daughter as he strives to 'reach something'. But perhaps the greatest sufferer from this failure of understanding will ultimately be Jimmy himself.

But if Barbara fails to open his eyes in this area, she succeeds in another: she finally brings him to the kind of meditation experience which Jimmy had found so elusive on retreat (pp.61–62). Her company also produces a sense of innocent wellbeing in Jimmy:

> It was nice, sittin in the kitchen, cosy. She lit caundles every night and we'd sit there wi some classical music on the CD. She never talked aboot herself much, nothin personal, just aboot meditation or the work she was daein or asked me aboot ma job. (p.59)

Far from being exhausted by the daily commute from Glasgow to Edinburgh, Jimmy is seemingly energised:

> Seemed tae have loads a energy – no mad, jumpin aboot energy, just feelin right in masel, kind of peaceful and centred. (p.59)

Even the commute in bad weather takes on its own charm:

> All the way alang the motorway it was beautiful. Even in the daurk you could feel the cleanness of the night, then, just outside Glesga a smirr of rain started and ah pit on the windscreen wipers. Rain, hame. Ah sterted tae smile tae masel. Rain, hame. (p.65)

Barbara, however, unwittingly sows an idea in Jimmy which will in due course lead to the central crisis in the novel: she indicates that she abstains from meat, alcohol and sex since she feels all three have a negative effect on her:

> 'I find I have more clarity if I just ... abstain from these things.' (p.64)

For Barbara, who lives alone, this regime affects only herself; Jimmy, however, is a family man and any such abstentions will have repercussions on people other than himself. When Jimmy puts this idea into practice we shall see the already tense situation at home becoming explosive.

For the moment, however, on his return, attention moves to the fancy dress party for his brother's fortieth birthday. For this Jimmy revisits his punk rocker past and spent time:

> [...] dancin and talkin tae folk ah hadnae seen for years [which] is thirsty work so ah was knockin back the pints. (p.72)

He eventually takes to the dance floor with his brother for a track from their youth and after a wild dance they collapse in a drunken heap, unaware that their antics have been filmed by camcorder. The rest of the family find his dancing and 'mooning' performance hilarious, as he would have himself at one time:

> [...] if ah hadnae been meditatin ah'd probly have got pissed and we'd all have had a good laugh aboot it the next day. (p.80)

But to the new Jimmy the idea of Anne Marie seeing her father in this drunken state disgusts him:

> 'Ah don't want ma wee lassie seein me like that. And ah don't want anybuddy else tae see it ever again.' (p.77)

So, taking a pair of scissors, he destroys the master tape of this significant family event, thus precipitating a major family row. Unable yet again to talk to a bewildered Liz about his feelings, he takes himself off to the Rinpoche, his spiritual adviser, to try to understand himself. He is impatient with the fact his meditating is having no noticeable improvement in the way he lives his life (p.80). The Rinpoche attempts to help him understand this self-disgust by suggesting parallels between meditating and getting a room ready for decorating:

> 'The meditation process is one of clearing [...] And it can get very messy for a while. But if we don't do it we don't ever get clear.' (p.81)

The Rinpoche invites Jimmy to examine his feelings towards the people that mean most to him and it is clear that there is a certain 'messiness' in his relationships: he feels he must appear 'like an eejit' to Anne Marie; he senses 'a gap' opening up between him and Liz; he is ashamed that he and his brother can only say they love each other when they are drunk. How then can he 'get clear' to be a better person? What form will the clearing take?

One method might have been to discuss his present unhappy state of mind with the people who matter most to him, in an attempt to let them understand the depth of his commitment to this new departure in his life and to seek their advice on how best to improve their damaged relationships. As we shall see, however, he will keep his own counsel, preferring to eradicate somewhat drastically all those elements in his life which he feels are impeding his desired 'clarity', without any consideration of the effect this will have on all their lives.

At the Retreat he had failed, apparently, to appreciate the implications of the Buddhist tenet that:

> 'Truly being in the present encompasses both the past and the future. You have to hold them all together as one.' (p.35)

Now, instead of acknowledging that previous errors and excesses were simply part of his past and 'encompassing' them into his present, he will seek rather a radical break with past behaviour, distancing himself from much of what made him the vital, likeable man he undoubtedly is. Such rash action in search of 'clarity' does not bode well for his, or his family's, future happiness. As we shall see, the 'messiness' will only get worse.

'Ah'm on a journey and ah don't know where ah'm gaun' (pp.83–151)

When Anne Marie resumes her narrative, we learn that communication within the McKenna household is suffering in the light of recent events:

> Ma mammy's no speakin tae ma daddy. Ma Uncle John's no speakin tae ma daddy. Everybody's speakin tae me but naebdy's tellin me anything. Happy faimlies. (p.86)

Family life is breaking down:

> Ah've hardly seen ma da, wi him workin all hours and spendin hauf his time at that Centre. (p.86)

Anne Marie feels increasingly isolated:

> And Ma used tae be dead interested in how ah was daein at school [...] But recently she's been gaun round in her ain wee world. (p.86)

Importantly, Anne Marie confirms that Jimmy's efforts to 'get clear' have already started:

> Ma da's changed. Ah mean at first it didnae seem tae make much difference tae him – even though he was meditatin he was the same auld da. [...] But noo, he's different. Dead serious. Says he's a vegetarian. Mammy's havin tae make two dinners every night, wan for him and wan for us. And he's stopped drinkin. (pp. 86–87)

In addition to her family woes, in the process of growing up, Anne Marie feels herself growing away from her best friend at primary school, Charlene, but again, the new atmosphere at home inhibits her discussing school problems with her mother in the way she once did. Previously, when a problem arose:

> [...] ah tellt ma mammy aboot it and it got sorted oot. And ah wanted tae talk tae her noo but how could ah? Everythin was different. Weird. (p.94)

Offsetting this gloom at home is Anne Marie's involvement with the school musical, *Joseph and his Amazing Technicolour Dreamcoat*, in which she has a part. This brings her into contact with a new Sikh friend, Nisha. This friendship is fostered by their both having parts in the musical and Anne Marie is increasingly to be found at the Singh household where the warmth she encounters there contrasts with chilliness at home.

> And it was cool gaun round tae Nisha's [...] And the food was great. Spicy, but no the way food in Indian restaurants is. Always straight off the stove or oot the oven. It was great

tae leave the school on a wet day and go round tae Nisha's hoose, sit at the kitchen table wi her while her ma served up wer dinner, the radio on in the background or a tape of Indian music. It was like when ah was wee and me and Charlene used tae go round tae ma granny's for wer dinner, dead cosy, though the calendar on Nisha's wall was of Sikh temples, no scenes of Donegal. (pp.98–99)

Anne Marie merges easily into this warm atmosphere, exotic in some ways but familiar in others, comparing it, as she does, to the welcome she found in her own grandmother's home. This is a household where cultures merge rather than collide, as lately they have tended to do at the McKennas. Gurpreet, Nisha's brother, is a DJ and

'He likes tae mix tracks. [...] Gurpreet samples everything – he puts in Indian music, Bollywood songs, pop, hiphop, bhangra, everything.' (p.101)

Languages, too, are a similar amalgam. When Gurpreet arrives home he first addresses his sister in English, or rather Glaswegian Scots:

'How many times have ah tellt you no tae come in here?' (p.101)

But later:

[...] he started speakin even lower, in a language ah didnae unnerstaund but mixed up wi English words and Nisha was answerin him in the same way. (p.102)

Although Nisha and her sister usually speak English, Gurpreet values the contribution of Punjabi, seeing it as a positive advantage in his musical activities:

'[...] Gurpreet likes tae mix it [Punjabi] in, especially when he's DJin. Thinks it makes him a bit different fae the others.' (p.102)

But while Anne Marie is gradually finding a way to compensate for the changes that have overtaken her home since her uncle's birthday party, Liz's troubles only intensify when Jimmy, already abstaining from meat and alcohol, announces he now wishes to become celibate for a period:

> 'It wis efter John's party, ah got tae thinkin aboot givin things up. Ah felt that ashamed.' He spoke slowly as if he wis thinkin it oot as he wis speakin, starin intae the distance. (p.104)

As startling as the decision itself, is the way it is delivered. Staring into the distance, he seems unaware that so radical a change to his marriage might benefit from full and meaningful discussion with the other person concerned, rather than coming as a unilateral declaration. Liz reacts with predictable anger:

> 'And whit aboot my desires, Jimmy?'
> He never answered, just sat there lookin stupit. Ah felt the anger rise in me. Ah was tryin tae be patient and listen tae him, but when he got thon look in his eye, he just went on his ain sweet way, payin nae heed tae anybody else. (p.104)

Jimmy's selfishness is self-evident and Liz, in her shocked anger, misses the opportunity to air the matter more thoroughly, interrupting him when he comes at all close to giving his reasons for explaining why this is important to him. Equally evident here, too, is the fact that Jimmy is attempting to follow Barbara's model for 'clarity', but he has failed to remember that she is single and he is married: there are implications for his marriage and his wife, as well as for himself, in abstaining from sex. He also appears not to have understood the oblique warning Barbara gave about trying to 'reach something' rather than trying to be 'fully aware in the day to day'. Were he to be so, he would surely be aware that his 'progress', as he defines it, is farcically trivial when placed beside the thirteen year marriage he is placing in jeopardy by driving forward in this insensitive manner:

> 'Nae drinkin, nae eatin meat. And wee things too – wan thing each day, know, just daft stuff. Say ah feel like a Kit-Kat wi ma tea but don't have wan or ah get a good tip fur a horse but never pit the line on, and, you know, ah feel as if ah'm makin some kindy progress.' (p.104)

Jimmy is a man confused and Liz a woman frustrated, but one not without ingenuity in attempting to rescue her conjugal life. Confident at first of the strength of their mutual physical attraction, she is surprised by Jimmy's persistence in his celibacy. Undaunted, she sets out to seduce him by organising a romantic candle-lit meal but to little avail:

> [...] ah don't usually pit on a short skirt and full warpaint just for wer tea on a Friday night. But he just looked at the flooers on the table and the candles and said, 'That's nice, hen. Have ah got time for a shower afore ma tea?' (p.106)

Further advances reveal that Jimmy may well have sexual feelings for his wife but he continues to ignore them to Liz's humiliation, explaining that:

> 'Ah'm on a journey and ah don't know where ah'm gaun.' (p.108)

Wherever his clumsy steps on this 'journey' are leading him, they are certainly distancing him ominously from his wife and, as we saw earlier, from his daughter and brother.

Unlike Anne Marie, Liz is unable at the moment to find comfort elsewhere. In addition to her problems with Jimmy, she is fully stretched at work, concerned by the failing health of her mother, exhausted by the housework of two households and guilty about spending so little time with Anne Marie. Just when Liz is feeling at her lowest, John's wife, Tricia, announces her pregnancy – and Liz's undiscussed desire to have another child re-emerges and with it news that she has had two miscarriages in the past, cruelly forgotten by Tricia.

This longing for a child is now all the more bitter when set beside her sister-in-law's pregnancy and the fact that Jimmy has discontinued marital relations.

> It was the thought of the new wan growin inside her that was gettin tae me. And the thought that, the way things were between me and Jimmy, what chance was there for me tae have another wean? (p.113)

But as well as falling short in his duties as a husband, Jimmy is, around now, also distracted from his duties as a father. On the night of the performance of *Joseph,* Jimmy announces he is attending a talk by Lama Thonden, 'an enlightened bein' who is 'ower fae America'. This cuts little ice with a furious Liz whose pent-up emotions tumble out as she sits at the performance, fuming to herself:

> Thon man. Ah couldnae get over just how selfish and self-centred he was. Him and his bloody Buddhism. Sittin there night efter night gazin at his navel and no seein anythin that was gaun on round aboot him. Him and his clarity. Clarity! If he'd open his eyes he might have some clarity. (p.115)

The rage of many weeks finds its main focus, interestingly, not principally on all the problems she herself has had to face herself with the new Jimmy, but on the snub to his daughter. But furious as she is with him, she later lies to Anne Marie to protect his standing with his daughter. (p.117)

Her remark above regarding clarity is worthy of note, for a second visiting lama will later make a rather similar remark to Jimmy:

> He was talkin aboot how we're all enlightened really but hauf the time we don't realise we are. Accordin tae him all we have tae dae is wake up and realise it. (p.167)

The comic irony here is that Liz, no friend of Buddhism, should be in agreement with this 'enlightened bein' on a central truth which for much of the novel escapes her doggedly Buddhist husband.

Once home, Jimmy is ecstatic about a pea which the lama had blessed. Perhaps not surprisingly:

> That night Jimmy slept in the spare room for the first time. (p.119)

Christmas sees a softening in Liz's attitude. She and Anne Marie attend midnight mass together and Liz's normal agnosticism is penetrated by the mood of the moment. She reflects on her treatment of Jimmy in a way she never has done before:

> Maist of the time ah don't actually feel that ah'm prayin or that there's anybody listenin tae me. But that night, sittin efter communion, when it was quiet and the priest was tidyin everythin away on the altar, as ah watched the figure of Jesus on the wall ah did pray; fae somewhere inside me came a feelin so strong that all the anger ah felt for Jimmy evaporated. Ah loved him, he loved me and it wasnae all his fault anyway. Ah'd been that tired and moany-faced recently ah'd never tried tae unnerstaund how things were for him. (p.125)

Later, as she cuddles into him in bed, she admits to herself:

> Ah needed tae talk tae him wioot gettin angry, try tae listen tae him, unnerstaund whit this wis all aboot. (p.126)

For the first time in the novel there is a glimmer of hope that this vitally necessary and long-delayed discussion will actually take place. She admits to herself that the present tattered state of their marriage is not all Jimmy's fault; she will try to see Jimmy's side of things, patch things up and

> If we could get wer act thegether ah could get pregnant again. (p.125)

Like many in her position before her, she sees a baby as the salvation of the marriage:

> A baby. Ah wanted a baby. And a baby would bring us back thegether. (p.125)

But that discussion never takes place. Jimmy is difficult to pin down since, to Liz's surprise, he announces he is using the Christmas break to paint the Centre. Her new-found restraint prevails, however, and she bites back the temptation to fly off the handle as before. On the rearranged date for their planned discussion her mother falls ill and the arrangement is cancelled. The millennium approaches without any sorting out of their relationship.

Millennium night, the central point in the novel's time-scale, sees the McKennas divided in several ways. Anne Marie, fresh from her success in *Joseph*, is invited with Nisha to take part in Gurpreet's millennium karaoke night and they score quite a hit as the Millennium Babes (pp.131–134). Liz, by contrast, finds herself alone and miserable at Tricia's celebration:

> Ah felt as if there was a bubble round me, ah was imprisoned in it, couldnae see through it properly; everythin was fuzzy and naebody could touch me. (p.135)

She is alone, since Jimmy, setting up yet another break with his past, has announced the pointlessness, as he sees it, of celebrating New Year at the traditional family party, now he has become teetotal; she is miserable, since it was on New Year's Eve six years ago that she had a miscarriage, a fact which seems forgotten and unmentioned by everyone around her, and which cuts her off even more from the festivities. Jimmy, somewhat typically, sees this family celebration from only his own point of view, with little thought of how his wife (has he, too, forgotten the miscarriage?) and family will react to this break with family tradition:

> How could ah tell her that ah just don't feel that way any mair, cannae be bothered wi the noise and the people, cannae

haundle it? Anyhow ah don't drink noo and whoever heard of seein in the New Year wioot a drink in yer haund? (p.140)

Interestingly, although he cannot talk to Liz about this, he does talk about it to the Rinpoche, who advises meditation as an alternative. The millennium sees Jimmy alone with a yellow candle, a statue of the Buddha, a CD of Tibetan chants and a photo of the Rinpoche. Advised again by the Rinpoche 'to do a bit of clearing' before embarking on meditation, Jimmy reveals that the abstention from meat, alcohol and sex has so far done little to help in the 'getting clear' process he has been involved in for some time now:

[...] ma mind was a complete and utter midden – a right guddle a thoughts and feelins fleein aboot aw ower the shop. (p.142)

Prominent amongst his thoughts is the realisation that Liz and he seem to be further and further apart:

And ah didnae know whit tae dae. Ah knew she didnae unnerstaund whit was gaun on wi me, ah didnae unnerstaund it masel. She'd be happy if we just went back the way we were, if ah gied up the Buddhism. But ah know ah'm no gonnae, no the now, no afore ah've got masel sorted. That's the bottom line. Ah've got tae keep gaun, see where it's takin me, hopin that at the end of it, somehow it'll be better for us all. (p.143)

Jimmy's journey has seemingly left him stranded in the middle of nowhere: he does not know what is happening to him, nor is he any wiser as to where this journey might be leading – despite the thorough-going changes he has already made to his life. He seems oblivious to the fact that it is his method of 'getting sorted' that is in fact the cause of much of this unhappiness, nor does it occur to him that discussing with Liz their joint problems might be one way to tackle this. Ominously, the only route he sees out of this difficulty is stubbornly ploughing on with the process that is already tearing his family apart.

Acknowledging his problems seems, however, to bring Jimmy some kind of relief and his meditation succeeds, bringing him peace for the moment at least. He meditates his way into the third millennium, awaking the next day with a heightened sense of the beauty of the world around him:

> Everythin in the room looked brand new. The colours on the downie cover, a pattern a yella and orange flooers, wis like sumpn in a movie it wis that sharp. Ah lay there fur a minute, just lookin at it. Just lookin. So this wis whit it wis all aboot. Just lookin. Just eveythin being clear. The light comin in the windae. En-light-enment. Seein the light. Ah'd seen the light. (pp.143–144)

Feeling good that enlightenment has seemingly come to him, he takes himself off to the Botanics where he wanders around, mesmerised at the beauty of the snowy landscape:

> Ah walked through the park, just full of it; the meditatin, the light, the snaw. Aw the bad stuff wis gone. Everythin wis gonnae be all right. Ah'd go up tae the hoose, get Anne Marie and Liz and bring them oot here intae the snow. (p.144)

Here we see the naivety of Jimmy. Admittedly, he *is* delighted by the beauties of nature, but Jimmy, we know, is a man with a strong appreciation of visual beauty anyway. And might not a good night's sleep have something to do with his new-found optimism? And might not that new-found optimism that *aw the bad stuff wis gone* be a little hasty? Would Anne Marie and Liz agree with him in seeing the beauty of the snow-covered Botanics as evidence that their family problems were solved?

Gone for the moment, however, are the doubts of the night before; for Jimmy, this is journey's end: enlightenment. In one of the great comic scenes of the novel, the author has this newly 'enlightened' being abruptly recalled to reality:

> Ah'd brung a bag a nuts fur the squirrels [...] So there am ur, daein ma St Francis a Maryhill act, convinced ah'm

Buddha Da

> noo an enlightened bein. And a wee squirrel hops ower the path, runs up ma leg oantae ma airm and afore ah can say Rinpoche, the wee bastard looks me straight in the face, bites me in the finger and runs aff. The blood's pourin ooty me, ah feel as if ah've been savaged by a bloody wolf, no a fuckin squirrel. Ah cannae believe it. It wis the way he just looked at me, just looked, as if tae say, 'up yours, pal'. (p.145)

This clearly is not yet true enlightenment, more of an anticlimax. Jimmy is still far from journey's end. He is indignant that a mere squirrel's bite (and a trip to the Western Infirmary) can puncture his illusion of the end to his problems, leaving him as confused as he was the night before:

> Ah mean, how come ah'd had this amazin experience, aw that clarity, just like it says in the books, and then wan wee thing, a squirrel for fuck's sake, a squirrel bites me and it's gone, as if nothin had happened. Ah just couldnae see it. It makes nae sense. (p.146)

More trouble awaits at home: Liz, exhausted by events leading up to the festive celebrations and exasperated by Jimmy's behaviour during them, reacts badly to a phone-call from Barbara, and subsequently accuses him of having had an affair with her. The accusation is only half-hearted, merely an expression of her bewilderment and anger with Jimmy's behaviour. While Jimmy may not have reached the end of the journey he had set himself, it is certainly the end of the road in one sense:

> He slept in the spare room that night, then the next day he packed a few things in a holdall and went tae stay at the Centre. (p.149)

Typically in this family, where there is scant discussion of important issues, the rupture is wordless:

> We never actually talked aboot him gaun. (p.149)

Initially, Liz feels that the separation will be short-lived, and is surprised by her dominant emotion:

> [...] there was wan less thing ah had tae think aboot [...] all ah felt was relief. Even though he hadnae taken any of his stuff away at first, it was as if the hoose was bigger wioot him, as if ah could breathe easier, had mair air. (p.150).

As time passes this emotion intensifies:

> And ah realised, aboot two weeks efter Jimmy had left, that ah was actually quite enjoyin it. Sounds daft, ah know, but somehow ah felt mair free wioot him. (p.151)

More surprises lie ahead. The McKennas are now entering uncharted waters; although married for thirteen years, Liz and Jimmy have enjoyed an intense relationship since Liz was fourteen. Such a break sees both Jimmy and Liz facing adult life alone for the first time. Anne Marie is entering adolescence without the joint support of her once close parents. While Jimmy may return regularly to see Anne Marie, the family is now facing an unexpected reconfiguration. How all three will fare in this new state of affairs constitutes the focus of the next section of the novel.

The fragmenting family (pp.153–205)
Up to the millennium celebrations, the McKennas were a family facing crisis, but one still functioning under one roof. After the new millennium, the novel follows their progress as they go their separate ways, with varying degrees of success and happiness.

Anne Donovan first explores how the new state of affairs affects Anne Marie. Although her father still visits regularly and her relationship with her mother seems to have improved (p.158), there is no denying her upset at the new situation. But it is to Nisha, and not to her own mother, that she confides her feelings and with whom she experiences the tearful outpouring of her pain at her father's departure, underlining once again one of the novel's major themes: the difficulty of discussing emotions within the family circle.

Faced with these new circumstances, we see Anne Marie's individuality further emerging. Unlike her mother, she makes attempts, through her school programme (pp.156–158) and her own visit to the Centre, to try to understand the doctrine that has so absorbed her father.

Anne Marie is not overly impressed by what she finds at the Centre:

> Everythin was clean but a bit shabby [...] (p.159)

and of the prayer room she comments:

> Ah looked round the room, tryin tae make some sense of whit ma daddy seen in all this, what had got tae him the first time he came here, but nothin happened. Ah didnae get it. (p.160)

Discovering her father is sleeping in a sleeping bag, she is even less impressed:

> Ah'd always assumed ma da had a room at the centre, but here he was, next door tae a dosser. (p.161)

Questioning her father about 'karma', she finds him as equally vague about Buddhism as he was at the beginning of the process:

> '[...] ah'm ur learnin aboot it right enough, but hauf the time ah don't ... well, it's just words, that's all.' (p.162)

Just as there was nothing in her school work that helped her understand why her father had left home, so, too, was there nothing in her visit which helped explain an attraction which had caused such an upheaval in all their lives. She leaves in an air of puzzled sadness.

After Anne Marie's departure, Jimmy feels a similar dissatisfaction. He wanders aimlessly round the Centre, knowing full well that this was probably a good time to get on with his meditating:

> But the last thing ah wanted tae dae was meditate. (p.164)

In the empty Centre Jimmy has all the peace he had once craved, but now it seems that disillusionment may be setting in. Tellingly, it is only when his thoughts turn to the mural he is planning for the Centre that his mood improves:

> Wanst ah started tae move the pencil alang the lines of the drawin, ah felt OK again. (p.165)

Here it is Jimmy's visual sensibility and his professional skills, seen previously at work in Edinburgh for Barbara, which bring him the contentment that Buddhist meditation singularly fails to do here. Another hint of disillusionment with Buddhism comes with the arrival of a visiting lama from France. An earlier visit from a visiting lama had left Jimmy ecstatic; now he reacts with irritation:

> Somehow it wisnae the same. He was talkin aboot how we're all enlightened really but hauf the time we don't realise we are. Accordin tae him all we have tae dae is wake up and realise it. And that sounded plain daft tae me. What was the point of daein all that meditation and all that if you're really enlightened all the time? (p.167)

Although Donovan handles Jimmy's rather jaundiced view of the event with humour, the lama's comments signal to the reader – above Jimmy's head at the moment – another of the novel's central ideas: being aware of the riches that already surround us is the secret of happiness, or enlightenment. In his quest to 'get somewhere', as Barbara put it, Jimmy has not been fully aware of the blessings of his family life; it will take later dramatic events in Liz's life to awake him to this. Even encountering his friend, Barbara, does nothing to put him in a better mood. So when Anne Marie later that day rents a Buddhist video to entertain him, he is not exactly responsive:

> But somehow, efter that ceremony and talkin tae Barbara, the last thing ah wanted was tae sit through a film aboot Buddhism. (p.169)

Life at the Centre – to say nothing of Buddhism – is proving less than fulfilling for Jimmy.

But while Jimmy and Anne Marie may be struggling to come to terms with his leaving home, Liz is entering an exciting new phase in her life.

Assisted by her friend from work, Nikki, Liz embarks on the social life of an adult single woman, something previously denied her by her association with Jimmy from the age of fourteen, as she herself admits:

> How can you know what you want when you're fourteen?
> Or twenty even.
>   Or thirty-three for that matter. (p.182)

While Jimmy is exploring his spiritual identity, rather unsatisfactorily, Liz is beginning to discover her social self, initially with some hesitancy:

> 'Less than a year ago ah thought ma life was all mapped oot, ah knew where ah was gaun, noo anythin could happen.' (p.176)

The reader, too, is beginning to discover the personality of Liz, the woman, rather than Liz, the wife and mother. On her first social outing, she encounters David Cameron, a twenty-six-year-old graduate student in Philosophy. (Interestingly, Liz, the most practical of women, finds herself involved in the course of the novel with two men who, in their very different ways, are engaged in philosophical pursuits.) In her conversations with him, Liz reveals the uncertainties she entertains about who she really is. Talking of her job she comments:

> 'It's almost like bein an actress, like it's no really me that does the job – ah play the part of an efficient organised secretary. Ah don't even talk like masel when ah'm at work.' (p.174)

Returning to the question of identity, she adds:

> Bein masel. There's lots of different ways a bein yersel ... ah'm wan thing at work and another at hame, or daein the messages or whatever. (p.174)

Without Jimmy around, she is obliged to seek out a new basis of identity; when David asks her if she is 'a party girl', she replies:

> 'Tae tell the truth, ah don't think ah know. Ah used tae be right intae gettin dressed up and gaun oot, loved dancin. But it's that long since ah've been on ma ain that ah just don't know any mair. [...] Ah know who ah am at work and wi Anne Marie and ma mammy ... but noo that Jimmy's no around ...' (p.176)

Whatever certainties she may have as to her identity, they all involve her social role as employee, mother and daughter; who she is as a woman remains to be discovered, a process which she will explore with David. They meet first at a party and then accidentally in the street. After they arrange to meet again, Liz returns to work and

> [...] all of a sudden a big smile spread across ma face. He'd asked me tae go and have a coffee wi him. No a date or anythin like that, but he must of wanted tae talk tae me, enjoyed ma company, a young guy like that, a Philosophy student. (p.177)

This pleasant process of discovery, however, is rudely interrupted by the death of Liz's mother, whose poor health has been troubling Liz for some time. The death is doubly upsetting to Liz since they had parted on bad terms when Mrs O'Sullivan had pointed out that Jimmy's love for her could not be doubted and that it was only Liz's pride that was stopping her asking him to come back. This comment sparks Liz's anger for she realises that there is more to this than her pride:

Buddha Da 35

> Then it dawned on me why ah was so angry wi ma mammy. She said ah was stubborn, didnae want tae make the first move. She said that Jimmy would come back if ah asked him tae. Well, mibbe she was right. And in ma heart of hearts ah didnae actually want him back. (p.181)

This realisation shocks Liz:

> [...] but in ma hert ah knew ah was enjoyin bein on ma ain. (p.182)

For the moment, however, guilt overcomes her surprise at the discovery:

> An hour ago, less than an hour ago, she'd been tellin me tae make it up wi Jimmy, and noo. It was ma fault. It was that fight wi me that made her take the heart attack or whatever it was that killed her. And the last words ah said tae ma mammy. What were they? 'Its no gonnae be me', words said in anger, slammin the door behind me. (p.185)

Personal discovery and guilt alike are put aside for the funeral preparations. This crisis sees a temporary coming together of the McKennas, subtly suggesting that the bond between them is deeper than their divisions when faced with a crisis. The individual paths they have been following are briefly interrupted as they face up to death in the family.

Jimmy, normally not the most practical of men around the house, proves a tower of strength when Liz's brother, Paul, goes to pieces in the organisation of the funeral arrangements in Mrs O'Sullivan's home. They work as a team, the 'we' and 'us' pronouns underlining their solidarity:

> Efter we'd moved the furniture, washed the dishes and tidied up we stood in the hall thegether. 'Is that us?' said Jimmy. (p.192)

Liz herself notes Jimmy's contribution:

> Jimmy stayed tae the end. It hadnae seemed strange at the time but noo ah'd time tae think aboot it it struck me how, when there was a crisis, it was as if we hadnae split up. (pp.192–193)

On the eve of the funeral, Liz and Anne Marie pay their final respects to the grandmother with Anne Marie singing the *Salve Regina,* taught her by grandmother, which she later sings at the funeral itself to great acclaim.

The scene at Mrs O'Sullivan's flat when the family arrive to say the rosary sees Donovan's talents as a novelist at their most subtly complex. It comes between two scenes of great emotional intensity – Liz and Anne Marie's farewell to Liz's 'mammy' in her coffin and the actual funeral itself – both of which are narrated by Liz. Between them comes this episode narrated by Anne Marie which, despite the sombre surrounding atmosphere, must count as one of the great comic scenes in modern Scottish fiction. Yet at the same time it is of key importance thematically and for the development of the characters of Jimmy, Liz and Anne Marie.

In inserting a comic scene to relieve momentarily the tension brought about by strong emotional pressures, Donovan is following in the steps of writers through the ages. As the entire family gathers, Uncle Paul, Liz's brother who has been of little help in the preparations, arrives, clearly very drunk, just at the same time as 'the wee man fae the St Vincent de Paul who led the rosary'. Shortly afterwards, Jimmy arrives with three lamas, which now rather overcrowds the premises. As Anne Marie comments:

> Mammy was just comin oot the livin room with the wee man and the lobby was suddenly stowed oot wi bodies. (p.199)

A confrontation arises between a furious Liz, outraged at what she sees as Jimmy's tactlessness in bringing his Buddhist friends to a Catholic ceremony, and a bemused Jimmy who, as usual, sees matters only from his own well-meaning but thoughtless perspective. As the friction mounts in the lobby, the drunken Paul appears, 'swayin fae side tae side in the livin room door':

> 'You go ... or else ah'll ... ah'll ...'
> He squared up tae ma daddy, who was aboot six inches taller than him, then bent ower and boked all over ma daddy's feet.
> Then he stood up straight again and carried on talkin as if nothing had happened, '... make ye go.' (p.200)

As Jimmy and Liz face up to each other in the lobby, each flanked by representatives of different religions, the comedy of the situation should not blind us to its key importance in relating each of them to one of the novel's key themes – how to engage with change. Liz's never distant hostility to Jimmy's preoccupation with Buddhism finds full expression here. Introducing the lamas to pray for her mother at the moment of the rosary is to her downright offensive:

> Mammy's face was like fizz. 'What the hell did you bring them here for?' (p.199)

She rejects out of hand Jimmy's well-meaning new slant on the rosary, reacting with uncomprehending fury to a seemingly disrespectful change to a traditional ceremony. While Liz may reject change here, Jimmy is also clearly guilty of introducing it somewhat clumsily, without consultation with other members of the family at this most emotionally fraught moment. (He claims, somewhat unconvincingly, to have mentioned bringing them, but Liz appears to have no recollection of this.)

This brief scene graphically illustrates the reasons for the breakdown in their relationship elsewhere in the novel: Liz maintains a bewildered hostility to the change Jimmy is introducing into their lives, while Jimmy engages with change in a muddled way, never fully appreciating the effects his altered behaviour and ideas are having on others close to him. One rejects change outright; the other engages with it clumsily.

But while Liz and Jimmy are playing out in the lobby the underlying reasons for their marital problems, Anne Marie is engaging with change in a wholly different manner. Forgotten in the heat of the row, she slips into the room with her grandmother's coffin where the lamas, oblivious to the drama their presence has generated, are chanting. Warming to the strange new sound of their chanting, she comments:

> As though they were musical instruments and the music was comin through them. And the sounds they made, that at first seemed harsh and discordant tae me, had become the maist beautiful sounds ah'd ever heard. Ah sat there and closed ma eyes. (p.201)

Earlier, sharing in some ways her mother's pained bewilderment at her father's engagement with Buddhism, she had left the Centre somewhat disconsolately, having failed totally to understand the attractions of Buddhism. Now, through her own musicality, she is beginning to open herself to its sensory appeal. Later, she will integrate its Tibetan sonorities into the Catholic *Salve Regina*, thus giving the novel a model for integrating change into tradition successfully, a feat which seems at the moment to be wholly beyond her warring parents.

But peace of a kind awaits Liz at the funeral itself. Here she admits to no great religious faith herself (p.204) but the familiar, traditional hymns (together with the large turnout of friends and family to pay their last respects) bring comfort. One untypical feature of this Catholic funeral (which momentarily outrages Liz) comes at the end of the service, when she spots the lamas joining in the hymns at the back of the chapel:

> And for a moment ah felt anger rise in me like a bitter taste – they'd no right tae be there [...] Then it faded as fast as it had come. They were only payin their respects. (p.205)

This note of acceptance towards the unfamiliar is a hopeful one on which to end this section of the novel, for Liz will have to reconcile herself to many more disturbances to her accepted norms in the months to come.

'You think that a funeral's the end but really it's the beginnin' (pp. 205–330)

With the departure of Jimmy and the death of her mother, Liz enters a strange new phase in her life, rather in the way that Jimmy had when he had discovered Buddhism. She calls it a 'beginnin'; Jimmy had called it 'gaun on a journey'. Both are embarked on explorations of aspects of themselves which their long relationship had kept them from examining. For Jimmy it is a spiritual quest; for Liz it is a discovery of her identity as an independent woman, freed as she now is from the role of daughter and wife. Helping her discover this new identity is David, the young man she had met through Nikki before the death of her mother. It is to David she turns for comfort and it is with him she sheds the first tears for her mother:

> Ah don't know if it was his voice, he just sounded that sympathetic and genuine, or if it was the shock comin hame tae me, but ah found masel startin tae greet, there and then in the middle of the crowded café, tears rollin doon ma cheeks, big sobs shudderin through me. (p.207)

As well as a shoulder to cry on, David is the person to whom she begins to talk about the guilt she feels about her mother, parting from her as she did in anger.

Confiding in non-family members seems to be a trait of the McKennas. We noted how Liz felt unable to talk about her innermost feelings to Jimmy while he was around; Jimmy confided his thoughts and concerns to Barbara and the Rinpoche; Anne Marie in her turn felt she could only talk about her worries to Nisha. Like Anne Marie before her, this inability disturbs Liz:

> All the time there was this big hole in ma life and naebody was talkin aboot it. (p.214)

But, as ever, Liz does nothing to remedy the matter with

her family. While discussions with David seem to soften the pain a little, it returns with a vengeance as she empties her mother's flat (pp.223–224). Her guilt is redoubled as she remembers how she had often resented looking after her mother in her later years. Long, bitter reflection on what she feels is her shameful past behaviour drives her to seek change, rather as it did Jimmy when the camcorder tape brought him face to face with what he, too, felt was his own regrettable behaviour of a rather different kind. Like Jimmy, Liz, too, seeks to put the past behind her; her solution is to banish her inner strife by re-making her outer self, announcing to her hairdresser:

'Ah'm a bit fed up and want a change.' (p.225)

Jimmy's desperate desire to distance himself from a distasteful self-image, drove him into somewhat rash behaviour that destabilised and imperilled his family life. Liz, a very different character and in very different circumstances, curiously, will follow his example. But while Jimmy renounces sex, Liz embraces it: she embarks on a wild affair with David, astonishing herself with the sheer physical joy it brings her (pp.227–229).

For someone who has shown herself to be somewhat ill at ease with change, this sudden embracing of it might seem puzzling. On closer examination, however, it is understandable at one level: Liz has been starved of a normal sex life since Jimmy adopted celibacy and in this physical relationship she is able to forget the pain and guilt of her bereavement. But how thoroughgoing is the change? She is reluctant in the face of pressure from David to go public with their affair and even more reluctant for Anne Marie and Jimmy to be made aware of it. It as if by keeping the affair secret, there is no outward acknowledgment of change to her circumstances; she is as yet burning no familial bridges. But an affair which began partly out of guilt of one kind is building up a guilt of quite another as she struggles to come to terms with the idea of her affair going on underneath the nose of Jimmy and Anne Marie:

> Ah knew whit ah was daein wis wrang, and stupit as well
> [...] (p.253)

Anne Marie, too, is having to come to terms with death in the family. Haunted by the 'Salve Regina' and intrigued by a competition on television to produce a CD, she and Nisha embark on a project to combine the 'Salve Regina' with the Tibetan chants of the lamas for their entry. By 'sampling' or integrating the spiritual music of the East into the traditional religious music of the West, to bring about an entirely new artistic creation, Anne Marie is successfully managing new influences on her life in a way that defeats her parents. Hers is – literally – a harmonious blending of the unfamiliar with the familiar. The impact of Eastern elements on her Western life also brings her enormous happiness, in a way that it totally failed to do for her parents:

> It was brilliant – actually it was the maist fun ah'd ever had [...] (p.243)

But as well as giving her pleasure her project with Nisha is also has another function:

> [...] it helped take ma mind aff ma granny. (p.243)

True to form, the McKennas fail again to discuss a matter of prime emotional importance with each other and Anne Marie, like her mother, turns to an outsider:

> The only person ah could talk to aboot it was Nisha. (p.243)

Although conducted in guilty secret, Liz's affair transforms her entirely for the moment. So absorbed is she by her affair with David, the normally cleanliness-obsessed Liz surprises herself at her acceptance of his rather messy student living arrangements:

> It was strange the way ah never minded the grubbiness of everythin. We'd lie in bed, talkin or no talkin, and ah'd

> watch the dust lit up in a sunbeam, the tangled-up socks in a corner of the room and just notice the way the colours blended intae each other. At hame ah couldnae of done that, ah'd of been oot ma seat cleanin the place up, but here it was time out. (p.251)

The question of how long this untypically relaxed attitude and behaviour of Liz's can last prompts itself to the reader as well as to Liz herself:

> But it couldnae go on like this. (p.253)

For Liz is someone who hates uncertainty and she is faced with a dilemma. What would be worse: telling Anne Marie what her mother has been up to and face the censure of her daughter or continuing to upset David whom she fears may end the affair, irritated by its furtive nature?

She is someone who, by her own confession, needs to know exactly what is about to happen in her life:

> [...] for me it's never today, it's always the morra. Every night ah look at the calendar and think aboot whit ah've got tae prepare for the morra, or next week. (p.256)

The organised side of her would like to see her life laid out before her from beginning to end, as if she were some astronaut looking down on it (p.256). Barbara had warned Jimmy of the dangers of trying to reach something without 'being fully aware in the day to day'. He had largely failed to recognise the wisdom of this Buddhist advice and had pushed on 'trying to get there, reach something' with destabilising results for him and his family. Liz, a very different character as she is in some ways, appears to be replicating his error:

> When ah grew up ah stopped livin fae moment tae moment, always too busy gettin somewhere. (p.256)

For she, too, undervalues the momentary pleasure of what surrounds her, feeling the need to be constantly looking to a targeted future. It is while mulling over this aspect of her personality that Liz indicates she is pregnant. Is falling pregnant her way of eliminating the current uncertainty in her life? Her series of questions to herself on p.256 suggest that she herself is confused as to how she came to find herself in this state. Was it an accident or did she will it subconsciously? As readers, we remember her long-held desire to have another child. Subtly, Anne Donovan leaves the matter open.

Whatever the reason, her pregnancy threatens to rock their already shaky family situation even more dramatically that Jimmy's obsession with Buddhism already has. While Jimmy may have been more overtly careless about the destructive effect of his obsession on the family as a whole, Liz's affair, while discreetly conducted and invisible to other family members as yet, risks even further the permanent fragmentation of the already damaged family unit. Her chief worry is how news of this extramarital affair and pregnancy would affect Anne Marie. The once cohesive McKenna family now risks being split even further apart by changes triggered by Jimmy and Liz exploring aspects of themselves as individuals rather than as family members.

While Liz is engaged in one form of creativity, so to speak, Jimmy, we learn, is engaged in quite another, as Anne Marie discovers when she, with her class, visits the Buddhist centre. Her father's mural of the Buddha, the one he had started when he had earlier felt depressed by his solitary life at the centre, dominates the meditation room impressively. Clearly, Jimmy is taking comfort in his rather forlorn lifestyle from the visual talents that had always been part of his professional self.

When we re-encounter Jimmy on p.263 he has been absent from the novel since the dispiriting experience of the French lama's visit, which in turn had followed shortly after his equally dissatisfying realisation in the Botanics that he was still a long way from the enlightenment he sought. A much more positive realisation strikes him when Liz answers the door to him: he finds her 'pure gorgeous'. Moreover, he is finding celibacy increasingly difficult, particularly when faced with this rejuvenated new Liz:

> Ah couldna look her in the eye – she must of known how ah was feelin. Ah wisht ah could just switch it aff, this feelin – no forever, just for the time bein, tae ah get things sorted in ma heid. But it doesnae work like that. At first when ah decided tae be celibate it didnae bother me – ah felt ah was controlling it, keepin ma mind on other things, but as time's went on it keeps comin back. (p.263)

The 'it' in question is a re-awakening interest in the wife he had so thoughtlessly sacrificed to his celibacy, the wife who is now engaged in an ardent affair with a younger man. Ironically, Anne Marie briefly suspects *him* of having an affair, with Barbara, when he invites her and Nisha to Barbara's flat in Edinburgh where he has work to do.

The trip to Edinburgh is a highly significant one. This brief journey was certainly not the one he had in mind when he had announced to Liz he was 'gaun on a journey' (p.108). Nevertheless it is the one which brings him far nearer to enlightenment than the other one ever did. He finds real joy in the simple joy of being with Anne Marie and her friend:

> [...] bright blue sky wi white puffy clouds and a sharp breeze blawin. Ah love days like that – it makes you feel alive. Ah felt that happy drivin through, the two lassies sittin up beside me in the van [...] (p.267)

The day goes on and the pleasure continues. They visit Arthur's Seat, at Barbara's suggestion, where Jimmy enjoys the sun while the girls turn cartwheels:

> Lyin on ma back wi the sun on ma face, eyes shut, listenin tae the girls laughin and bletherin away, ah felt happy. Just happy. Ah'd no felt this happy for a lang time. Just lyin in the sun. Then all of a sudden there was a feelin in the pit of ma stomach like when you're at the shows and you feel the big wheel fallin under you in a rush, like ma insides had been sooked oot of me. Ah opened ma eyes and it was all still there, the sun, the view ower Edinburgh and the hills, Anne Marie and Nisha a coupla foot away, sittin on the grass. (p.269)

Buddha Da

Later, alone in the meditation room, he mulls over the events of the day:

> That night, lyin in ma sleepin bag, watchin the light fae the cars spill oot under the curtains and move alang the skirtin board, that was whit was comin back tae me. Two lassies turnin cartwheels. And a blue and white sky. (p.270)

At long last, Jimmy has become 'fully aware in the day to day', as Barbara had long ago advised him to be (p.57). He is also experiencing the truth that the little-respected French lama had offered:

> He was talkin aboot how we're all enlightened really but hauf the time we don't realise we are. Accordin tae him all we have tae dae is wake up and realise it. And that sounded plain daft tae me. (p.167)

Jimmy has finally woken up to partial 'enlightenment' and become aware of *some* of the simple riches that surround him and of which he has been so careless of late. This vision of joy is created, not by some meditation-driven insight, but by the everyday sight of two girls turning cartwheels. But is his awakening too late? His wife, to whom he is again being drawn, is already pregnant by another man. Can he return to his once happy state and retrieve the riches he once shared with her, thereby completing his journey to a full awareness of his enlightened state?

As the novel nears its end, there is increasing emphasis on the life force: Tricia's baby, Roisin, is born and Liz awaits the arrival of her own baby. But first she has to break the news to David he is about to be a father.

In her imagination, Liz had already pictured a scenario for his reception of the news:

> And in ma heid he'd always take me in his airms and everythin would be all right. He was over the moon, overjoyed, couldnae wait. Even though it was too soon, a bit messy, we could make it alright. (p.277)

The reality is somewhat different. His reception of the news (pp.278–280) suggests he is far less enthusiastic, seeking refuge in what he says are the unfortunate timing of events:

> 'The timin. It's always the timin. Life, ah mean [...] If things come along at the right time, well, everythin's brilliant – but if it's the wrong time, it's a disaster [...] now if we'd met, let's say two year fae noo. Ah've finished the PhD and got a job, you've divorced Jimmy … perfect. Then efter a couple a year, you get pregnant. When we're ready.' (p.279)

Clearly, David is not ready, flirting even with the idea of abortion. Like Liz, he likes the idea of the future being mapped out, but this unplanned event has no place on his map. He reacts somewhat coolly. His uncertainty about the new situation grows:

> 'You know ah really like you, and if we'd time tae see how things developed … ah mean it could of worked oot.'
> 'So you're sayin they cannae work oot noo.'
> 'Naw, ah'm sayin that, mibbe they could, ah mean there's whit – seven month tae go – a lot could happen in seven month.' (p.283)

In brief, David, for all his continuing sexual ardour towards Liz, is less than wholehearted in his reception of the pregnancy and Liz herself is beginning to wonder if they are 'sustainable' as a couple (p.282). The pregnancy is not without its problems and Liz, who has suffered two miscarriages already, we remember, is fraught with worry. In her fearful state, she longs for someone to turn to:

> [...] ah wanted someone tae look efter me. And there was naebody. How come when the bleedin started ah never even phoned David tae see if he'd go tae the hospital wi me … it had never even crossed ma mind. (p.294)

At this low point, she encounters Jimmy at the flat who is solicitous of her strained appearance, makes her a cup tea, sits down beside her to comfort her, putting his arm round her and Liz begins to make comparisons:

> [...] he felt that different fae David, that solid. (p.295)

But the longed-for solid comfort that Jimmy offers, and which David had singularly failed to do, is short-lived. The announcement of Liz's pregnancy sends Jimmy off on a dark night of the soul. He reflects bitterly on his lot at the centre:

> Hame. A mattress on the flair in a corner of the prayer room. The prayer room. Ma mural. Ma project. Ma process. The mindfulness of. Breathin. Comin harder and faster noo. Hurtin ma chest. (p.297)

But the hurt is more than physical. Liz's announcement has brought yet another kind of enlightenment to Jimmy, but this new understanding is not the joyful kind which he had experienced at Arthur's Seat with the girls. There is real pain as he realises that he had a life which he had abandoned in favour of seeking 'clarity':

> Ah used tae have a life. Never thought aboot it tae ah met the Rimpoche. Just got up in the mornin and got on wi it. Work. Hame. Anne Marie. Liz. The stuff. (p.298)

He had wanted to understand more about life and in his quest for this he had lost the one he had – and a new one was in the offing in which he had played no part:

> But noo there's a new life. Growin inside Liz. And it's got nothin tae dae wi me. (p.298)

He now has a dearly-bought 'clarity' but his new understanding brings him only pain and in a fit of self-loathing he destroys his mural, thus symbolising his final renouncement of his flirtation with Buddhism which has so far brought him little and cost him seemingly everything.

Meanwhile, Liz and David spend a near perfect day at the seaside together where David announces he has been offered a place on an exchange programme to conduct his research in America. (We remember how at their last meeting Liz had been surprised by the tidying up which the usually untidy David had been doing, suggesting he had already been indulging in some forward planning.) Although David claims not to want to let Liz down (p.304), Liz senses his desire to be free and generously makes the situation easy for him by telling him:

> It's a big chance for you. There's nothin you can dae here. You have tae go. (p.307)

David has given Liz a great deal: great solace in every way after she found herself alone after the death of her mother and the departure of Jimmy. He has also given her her heart's desire – a baby – although the circumstances are proving fraught for Liz. But underneath, David is not the 'new man' he claimed to be (p.211). 'New' man David (in going to America) is pursuing his own interests rather in the way that the 'old' Jimmy used to.

But when Liz arrives home she is confronted with a 'new' Jimmy. The Jimmy who was once so thoughtless around the house is now 'puttin a casserole dish in the oven' (p.307) saying 'ah thought ah'd make masel useful' (p.307) so that Liz can keep her strength up.

His dark reflections have produced a more thoughtful man, one concerned for the woman he had treated so carelessly, although he feels he may have lost her forever. Liz appreciates the comfort of his presence:

> We sat at the kitchen table, two identical mugs in front of us. Sippin, tea, listenin tae the clock tick. Just the same as we had always been. Even though Jimmy didnae live here any mair it was just the way it had always been. But noo it couldnae stay the same, soon the bairn growin inside me would change everythin. (p.307)

Liz, like Jimmy earlier, appreciates that the family life they once enjoyed has been changed utterly by their individual actions. But the change is perhaps not all negative, for sitting together in the kitchen they begin to do what they have avoided doing for so much of the novel: they begin to discuss with each other – admittedly tentatively – their confused situation, with Liz inviting Jimmy back to the holiday cottage, booked before her mother's death. There is a hint, too, of more united action when Liz invites Jimmy to help her resolve a matter that has been concerning her for some time: how to tell Anne Marie about the baby:

> 'What aboot Anne Marie? Ah think we should tell her thegether.'
> 'Whatever you think.' (p.308)

Jimmy clearly has not lost entirely the life he once had and Liz has gained the support she longed for earlier (p.294). Jimmy, the tradesman, rather than Jimmy, the Buddhist, makes one last trip to the centre to paint over the mess he had made of his portrait of the Buddha, symbolically turning his back finally on the mess he had made of that part of his life.

Meanwhile, Anne Marie has completed her CD, her 'silver circle' (p.309) of Tibetan chants and *Salve Regina*, a feat that harmoniously brings together east and west in a way that her parents had failed so dismally to do. As the novel nears its close, Donovan foregrounds this idea of the circle: the cartwheels at Arthur's Seat, Anne Marie's CD, the coming together of Liz and Jimmy again, the return to the seaside cottage where the novel's central action had really begun. For some, this might suggest the Buddhist cycle of death, rebirth and renewal (the death of Liz's mother, the unborn baby) but in western literature the circle is also a potent symbol of completeness and wholeness. The McKennas began the novel as a strongly united family, fragmented under the stresses brought about by Jimmy's actions and finally find reconciliation. This reconciliation finds expression as Liz and Jimmy listen to Anne Marie's composition.

> Ah watched their faces as they listened the first time: ma daddy's wee smile as he recognised the lamas' chantin then, them lookin at each other as ma voice came in singin 'Salve Regina'. When it was finished ma daddy said, 'That's amazing, hen,' and Mammy gied me a hug and said, 'Well done.' (p.310)

The family circle is again nearly complete – but not quite. There is the new baby to be considered and Anne Marie still to be told. To Liz and Jimmy's consternation, she assumes Jimmy is the father and is delighted by the news, seeing this as a signal that Jimmy will be returning home permanently now. Her assumption makes telling her the truth of the baby's paternity even more difficult, but their problem leads to the frankest and fullest discussion they have ever had in the novel, but not before Jimmy, observing the pregnant Liz, suffers one more pang of regret:

> How could ah of let this happen? It was ma fault. If ah'd no been that blind, ah'd of known how much she wanted another wean ... and another wave of sickness as ah thought [...] and the bairn no mines. (p.324)

This pain leads him, however, to his most unselfish act in the novel: his acceptance of the baby as his own. In this post-Buddhist phase, he performs his most Buddhist act: he loses his own sense of self to seek to welcome another man's child into his home and acknowledge it as his own. Doubts remain. Will he be able to live up to this big-hearted gesture? The question is left open. It is one of the novel's great strengths that it does not seek too neat an ending to this complex relational dilemma, accepting the messiness of the family's situation. Quizzed by Liz who is concerned by the long-term implications of another man's child in the home, he, with great frankness, sums up their situation:

> But whatever we dae will be a mess. At least this way there's a chance we might all be happy. (p.325)

His love for Liz overrides the biological truth of the matter:

> It is mines [...] It'll be our wean, Anne Marie's wee sister or brother. (p.326)

There are no guarantees of success, however, but in accepting this, Jimmy, not normally the most articulate of men, delivers a powerfully moving declaration of love and commitment:

> All ah can say is that ah've loved you since ah was eighteen and ah still love you and ah think we should gie it our best shot. (p.326)

4. CHARACTERS

Jimmy

Interviewed by the *Barcelona Review*, Anne Donovan noted:

> [I gave] each of the characters a different dominant sense so that when I was that character then I concentrated on their way of viewing the world. Jimmy of course is visual.

This is evident in his trade as a house-painter. We remember how skilfully and almost lovingly he sets about decorating the intricate plasterwork of Barbara's Edinburgh flat, losing himself in the work entirely. When resident rather unhappily in the Buddhist centre, his one comfort comes, not from meditation, but from his visual sense, when he sets about drawing the outlines for a mural of the Buddha.

> Wanst ah started tae move the pencil alang the lines of the drawin, ah felt OK again. (p.165)

His eye for the beauty of nature and its attendant comfort comes to the fore again in his ill-fated outing to the Botanics under the snow and, later, when he visits Arthur's Seat with Anne Marie and Nisha.

In the same interview Anne Donovan adds to her view of Jimmy:

> Jimmy has a huge heart, he's instinctive, he is a big presence.

But while Jimmy's heart may be in the right place, his head tends to let him down. He has grave difficulties understanding the tenets of Buddhism and it is this which causes many of the problems of the McKennas. This is highlighted in his attempt to define karma to Anne Marie:

> 'Ah think it's like – when you dae sumpn and then sumpn else happens – it's meant tae be. Ma granny used tae say, "Whit's fur you'll no go by you." It's a bit like that.' (p.162)

Far from being something that is 'meant tae be', karma is the law of cause and effect: what we sow today, we reap tomorrow. Jimmy's pain and misery stem largely from his hasty and thoughtless actions of embracing celibacy and breaking with his past life without thinking through their consequences. He also seems unaware that enlightenment requires the surrender of the selfish desire to impose our own wishes on life if we are to be aware of the beauty and goodness that surrounds us: Jimmy's determination to follow his own will, despite the pain it is causing his family is thus further proof of his limited understanding of basic Buddhist ideas. It takes the painful realization that Liz's baby is not his to awaken him to the fact that he is the creator of his own unhappiness; that he had enjoyed a good life and had foolishly turned his back on it in his own wilful pursuit of 'clarity'. (p.298)

Ironically, the novel holds out the possibility that Jimmy may well end up a better Buddhist when he abandons the active pursuit of Buddhism than when he practised it. In his willingness to accept the baby, another man's child, into his family, he loses his preoccupation with 'self' and the self's desires that have temporarily taken over this big-hearted man.

Anne Marie

The similarities and contrasts with her father are striking. Like her father, Anne Marie is showing dissatisfaction with elements in her present condition as the novel opens. The early pages find them both feeling their present life requires some kind of change. She, however, does not provoke any radical break with her earlier life; she quietly accepts that one-time school friend, Charlene, is part of her past and works at exploring a new present with her Sikh friend, Nisha, and the world of music. Like Jimmy, she is open to other cultures, (note, too, her interest in world geography at school) but while Tibetan Buddhism poses various problems for Jimmy, Anne Marie is instinctively at home with the Singhs and draws a comfort and warmth from her Sikh friends and their life-style in a way which will later elude Jimmy when he moves into the Buddhist centre.

She shares her father's one-time interest in music, but while his musical tastes remain fixed in his punk-rocker past, hers are eclectic and open to new influences. Underlining this is her admiration for Madonna, an artist famous for her ability to change endlessly the presentation of herself. Anne Marie's CD brings together Catholic and Tibetan elements to create a new artistic synthesis. Her venture into creativity inspired by other cultures is far more successful than that of her father's, whose mural ends disastrously.

In short, Anne Marie is much more at home with change and is more adept at adapting to it than her father. To borrow Barbara's terms, we see that Anne Marie is not consciously reaching out to get somewhere, she is simply completely engaged in what she's doing musically and finding the exercise rewarding and fulfilling, as her growing happiness in her musical prowess demonstrates.

Liz

Liz is the practical one of the family: she holds down a responsible administrative post in a lawyer's office; she, not Jimmy, had calculated that buying their big three-bedroom flat would benefit the family's finances; she arranged the mortgage; she coped with running two households when her mother was ill; she was the family member who took charge of the funeral arrangements after her mother's death. Liz likes being organised and is much given to planning:

> Every night ah look at the calendar and think aboot whit ah've got tae prepare for the morra, or next week. Is there ironin tae be done, any messages tae get, dae ah need tae take sumpn oot the freezer for the morra's dinner? (p.256)

Nothing would make Liz happier than to see her entire life planned out:

> Ah wish ah could see ma life spread oot in front of me, as if ah was up in the sky; like an astronaut lookin at a river, seein the start and the middle and the end of it as it flows tae the sea. (p.256)

Change is the enemy of forward planning, so it is little surprise that Liz is increasingly hostile towards the strange developments that overtake Jimmy in his spiritual adventure and their disrupting effects on their previously stable family life.

But there is another side to Liz. In the *Barcelona Review* interview referred to earlier, Anne Donovan sees Liz's dominant sense as being her sense of smell, adding that she is also very sensual. Her sensuality is caught early on in the novel as she cavorts with Jimmy in the sea:

> [...] ah caught ma breath for a minute and shut ma eyes, feelin the cauld water and the heat aff the sun and the nearness of him all at once. (p.20)

In her affair with David she astonishes even herself with the sensuous intensity of the physical pleasure they enjoy together (pp.227–229).

Liz's sense of smell is one of Donovan's chief methods of characterising her. Different aspects of her personality find expression in a variety of smells:

> It's funny but when Liz is really mad aboot sumpn, she goes mental wi bleach. The place is honkin – you just follow the smell and there she is, rubber gloves up tae her oxters, scourin away [...] (p.40)

Hence Jimmy, on his return from the Buddhist retreat, knows that his visit has gone down extremely badly with Liz, alert as he is to the association of bleach and anger in Liz's universe. The bitter regrets and shame she feels at what she thinks were her grudging kindnesses to her mother in her latter days find similar olfactory expression when she returns to empty her mother's home:

> A sour smell hit me when ah opened the door. (p.220)

The sourness encapsulates not just the physical smell of disuse but the metaphorical scent of self-reproach as well.

But there is yet another scent in the house. Liz is made aware of time passing by the smell in her mother's wardrobe:

> Ah imagined the dry skin flakin aff ma mammy, powderin and workin itsel intae the folds of the claes. These claes hangin up here infused wi the skin of ma mammy, moulderin away inside this wardrobe [...] and ah smelled the scent of auld, auld skin. Ah wanted tae greet [...] (p.223)

For a woman longing to have a baby, this keen, scent-related reminder of the passing of time is not lost on Liz. Four pages later she is caught up in wild love-making with David.

But for Liz scents are not only associated with negative feelings: her sensuality expresses itself through fondness for delicate fragrances, too. Keen to make amends for his absence at the Buddhist retreat, Jimmy appeals to this:

> Ah'd bought a bunch a freesia and stuck them in a vase in the kitchen. It's Liz's favourite – she likes the smell. (p.43)

Perhaps the most complex personality in the McKenna household, Liz is torn uneasily for a time between exploring her individual sexuality and family values. She revels in the sensuality she enjoys with David but worries at the same what the impact will be on Anne Marie should she find out what her mother has been up to. Her pregnancy throws her into confusion; Liz, the great planner, has no plan for dealing with this eventuality. The once highly organised woman feels fragile and vulnerable in this new situation. David fails her in this state but Jimmy provides the support she craves (pp.307–308).

As in Jimmy's case, the messy exploration of individuality has resulted, belatedly, in a re-awakened appreciation of what their joint lives had given them in the past:

> We sat at the kitchen table, two identical mugs in front of us. Sippin tea, listenin tae the clock tick. Just the same as we always had been. Even though Jimmy didnae live here any mair it was just the way it had always been. (p.307)

This new baby, the result of a family split, paradoxically brings both Jimmy and Liz to a greater awareness of the value of their shared life, a value that their individual quests had temporarily overshadowed. In Jimmy's case, this new awareness results in a more caring, less self-centred human being; in Liz's case, we see her overcoming the pride her mother had accused her of (p.180) and making the first move in a reconciliation. The needs of family are put above personal ones and are what finally bring them together. She worries about what to tell Anne Marie with regard to the new baby:

> 'Ah think we should tell her thegether [...] ah know it's gonnae be a terrible shock for her, and she'll need us baith ...' (p.308)

With this realisation comes the invitation to Jimmy to rejoin the family by returning to the sea-side cottage with her and Anne Marie:

> '[...] would you come wi us? Then we could tell her when we're thegether [...]' (p.308)

In the final pages of the novel we see a less self-assured but more attractive Liz. She has not given up on wondering about the future, but she faces it now, not with plans, but with philosophical acceptance of its unpredictability:

> But what aboot the future?
> Wish there was some way of knowin if we're daein the right thing, but there isnae. Never is. (p.328)

5. THEMES

The difficulties of family communication

Excellent though the McKennas are in communicating with the reader, they are a good deal less impressive when it comes to communicating with each other. Whenever in the course of the novel they are faced with an emotional crisis, each one fails to bring his/her emotions into open family discussion, sharing rather their concerns with an outsider to the family circle.

Liz is a character with much on her mind as the novel opens: she is worried by Jimmy's new solitariness, her mother's failing health and nurtures a deep desire to have another baby after earlier miscarriages. These are all important issues to the well-being of the family which merit in-depth discussion with her husband, but this never happens, despite the close physical bond between her and Jimmy. After her mother's death, her pent-up emotions find outlet with a virtual stranger, David, with whom she shares her anguish, not just about her loss but the failure to discuss it:

> Mammy's no here. And naebody's talkin aboot it. (p.217)

Later, after her separation from Jimmy, when her relationship with David develops, she is similarly reluctant to discuss the matter within the family, preferring her work-mate Nikki as her confidante. Although Anne Marie is very much on her mind throughout this liaison, she avoids broaching the matter with her, saying:

> Ah need tae find the right time tae tell her. (p.234)

But the right time never seems to arise.

Jimmy is similarly reluctant to bare his emotions to his family. On returning from his retreat he seethes with indignation at what he sees as Liz's condescending attitude towards his interest in meditation (pp.41–42) but his feelings here (and Liz's, too, for that matter) are never declared. Bewildered by his own violent behaviour in cutting up the film of his brother's birthday party, he takes his troubles to an outsider, the Rinpoche. Here he reveals difficulties in his relationships with his wife, his daughter and his brother, but these difficulties are never broached by him in family discussion. (p.82) Barbara Mellis in Edinburgh is another outsider with whom he shares feelings never openly discussed with his wife, confessing to her tellingly:

> You know, Barbara, ah don't really know whit she [Liz] thinks. (p.64)

Nor does he really ask. Admittedly, as his exchanges with Anne Marie regarding his understanding of Buddhism demonstrate, he is not the most articulate of men, but the strength of his attraction to Buddhist meditation (and Liz's anger with the changes it is bringing to the family) might suggest the necessity of at least attempting an explanation of the importance of the subject to him.

Anne Marie is perhaps the chief victim of this failure of communication. As a twelve-year-old starting secondary school, she has her own concerns. Confused by the breakdown of her friendship with her friend Charlene from primary school and the silence that has grown up between her mother, father and Uncle John, she longs for meaningful discussion within her family, but none is forthcoming:

> Everybody's speakin tae me but naebody's tellin me anything. (p.86)

In pre-crisis times, this was not always the case, she tells us (p.86), but despite her willingness to talk to her mother in particular, she never has the chance. Instead, she takes her unhappiness to her new Sikh friend, Nisha, who, after Jimmy's departure from the family home and later, after the death of her grandmother, becomes her chief confidante:

> The only person ah could talk to aboot it was Nisha. (p.243)

The question arises why this warm-hearted family seems incapable of discussing matters close to the heart with each other. David's comments to Liz as he comforts her indicate that this is not a problem unique to the McKennas but one that is more widespread:

> That was the trouble wi ma faimly, we'd never been able tae talk aboot anythin, so when ma mammy died, it all just got swept under the carpet. (p.218)

Liz, herself, sees this inability as a matter of generational conditioning, of which she appears to be the result. Speaking of her mother, she comments:

> [...] ah suppose she'd loved us for it wasnae her way tae say it. Her and all her generation. They werenae brung up tae say they loved you. Ah wasnae brung up tae say it either. (pp.223–224)

And while she was once able to express her emotions to Anne Marie as a child, she seems, as she has grown older, to revert to her mother's behaviour. Once she could tell Anne Marie she loved her:

> Ah used tae say it every day when she was wee ... Always, then noo she's a teenager and when ah turn up at the school gate it's 'you should of phoned me.' (p.224)

Given the family reluctance to express what is closest to their hearts, it is no surprise that they are constantly misinterpreting each other's behaviour: they have only the outward signs by which to judge. Liz feels that Anne Marie is 'neither up nor doon aboot her daddy bein away' (p.150) but, unbeknown to her, Anne Marie, in tears, is pouring out her woes to Nisha (p.156). Jimmy feels Anne Marie is not 'that interested' in Buddhism (p.163) whereas she has gone to some lengths to inform herself about the subject to understand her father better.

It takes the crisis brought about by Liz's pregnancy to shock Jimmy and Liz into beginning to discuss their situation in a way they have avoided for much of the novel (p.307). In examining how best to tell Anne Marie about the paternity of the baby, their dialogue takes on a refreshing openness and directness which have been lacking until this point. In this dialogue their relationship is tenderly re-established. But Anne Marie never *does* get told the biological paternity of her new sibling. The reader may fear that this is a return to the bad old days when important family issues never got discussed, but the frankness of the exchanges between Liz and Jimmy (pp.324–326) dismisses any such charge. Their discussions bring them closer than they have ever been in the novel. Jimmy may now have renounced direct involvement with Buddhist activity but here he makes a truly Buddhist gesture: he loses all sense of himself in accepting another man's child as his own. Generosity triumphs over biology to the point that Jimmy can declare:

'It is mines.' (p.326)

If, as he says, he already feels it to be to be 'our wean', then there is no real revelation to be made. Are they making the correct decision in boldly blurring (or is it concealing?) the paternity of the child? Will Jimmy be able to live up to his generosity? The novel offers no neat solutions, preferring to leave the reader to decide.

Negotiating change

The world of *Buddha Da* is a world of change. It opens in one millennium and closes in another. The McKennas return in the final pages of the novel to the holiday cottage where the essence of their story could be said to have begun, but their world has changed significantly: the first visit was overshadowed by an impending death; the second anticipates the birth of a baby. The summer of 1999 saw them as a traditional family; in 2000 their family unit is approaching a reconfiguration as a result of actions by both Liz and Jimmy which could hardly be said to conform with the norms of traditional family life. Although the cottage may be the same, the McKennas who return to it are considerably transformed both in their circumstances and characters.

Change over the course of the intervening year has been negotiated with varying degrees of success by the three McKennas. Jimmy is the initiator of much of this change. His unilateral decision to practise celibacy at a time when his wife (unnoticed by him, it must be said) is longing for another child is inconsiderately done. He takes no heed of the changes his new lifestyle might have on anyone except himself. His preoccupation with Buddhism sees also the once thoughtful father change to one who prefers attending a Buddhist lecture to attending his daughter's school concert. The fracture of the once stable family unit which results finds the three McKennas thrown into unfamiliar territory in which they deal with the change in their own very different ways.

Jimmy's new life-style, once established, does not seem to bring him any real satisfaction as he struggles to comprehend the intricacies of Buddhist meditation practices in the spartan and lonely surroundings of the Buddhist centre. His well-meaning but clumsily executed idea of having Tibetan lamas participate in the traditional Catholic recitation of the rosary is one change too many for Liz, seriously aggravating, as it does, Jimmy's already strained relations with his wife. Although the instigator of change in the novel, he manages it thoughtlessly, resulting in unhappiness for not only Liz and Anne Marie but for himself also.

Liz is a highly organised woman for whom an orderly, planned life is essential. On p.256 she talks of her wish to see her life totally mapped out, 'seeing the start and the middle and the end as it flows tae the sea.' Surprises along the way such as Jimmy introduces figure nowhere in her plan and she reacts hostilely to the abrupt changes he precipitates. Admittedly, Jimmy has brought about changes insensitively without due regard to his role as husband and father, but Liz's resentment towards the changes in Jimmy also lacks reflection, as she herself at one point acknowledges (p.125). Once alone, however, she discovers that her feelings are those of relief as she explores her status as a single woman. There is no doubting the physical gratification her affair with David brings her and for a time she embraces this change as joyfully as she does the man himself. With her pregnancy, however, comes the realisation of her vulnerability and she longs for the security she once knew.

The conception of this baby is the final catalyst of change in the lives of both Jimmy and Liz, coming as it does at a time of crisis for both of them. Parallel with Jimmy's disillusionment with Buddhism is his realisation of his reawakened love for his rejuvenated wife. Parallel with Liz's acute sense of vulnerability is her realisation of the solid reliability of Jimmy in comparison with David. The awkwardness of their new situation – what to tell Anne Marie – is surmounted by the kind of frank dialogue that has been missing from their lives to date (pp.323–326). The baby has brought about the greatest change of all in their recent lives, and it is a change with which they engage with a maturity that neither of them has shown before. For Liz, the big change is to accept that the planned life she always wanted for herself is an illusion. Life's unpredictable nature has to be embraced, although part of her still longs for her old certainties:

> Wish there was some way of knowin if we're daein the right thing, but there isnae. Never is. (p.328)

For Jimmy the change is to become fully aware of the riches he almost lost by his inconsiderate behaviour towards the woman he always loved and could so easily have lost.

Anne Marie has to deal perhaps with more change than anyone in the family. There is, first of all, the move from primary to secondary school, with its realisation that we outgrow our old friends and have to make new ones. She has to deal, too, with the puzzling new behaviour of her father, the separation of her parents and the death of her grandmother. Although these changes cause her pain and bewilderment, she finds her own way to cope with them with a sureness that eludes her parents. She seeks comfort wherever she can find it and this is with Nisha and her family.

She seems instinctively at home with other cultures, as her effortless blending into the life of Nisha's family and her pleasure at the Tibetan chanting at the rosary well illustrate. Her openness to change allows her musicality to express itself confidently in the world of hit musicals, Madonna-inspired karaoke and Catholic church music. The latter she combines to great effect with Tibetan chants to create her successful CD, a harmonious synthesis of tradition and change.

Her success in managing change could well serve as a future model for the McKennas as a family group in this latest phase of their lives. Just as she successfully merged the unfamiliar with the familiar, so too will they have to manage a similar synthesis when the new baby arrives, if their family circle is to be as complete as it once was.

If, as *Buddha Da* seems to suggest, happiness depends to a large extent on how well we engage with change, then the new developments in Jimmy and Liz (pp.323–326) are promising. As they face together the arrival of Liz's love-child, Jimmy is more considerate, Liz is more tolerant. It is no coincidence that Donovan has this scene take place by the sea, itself the symbol of permanence yet constant regeneration. They both now manifest a new maturity in the face of change absent earlier from their personalities. This results in a willingness, albeit with some qualms, to accept an uncertain future as their best hope for happiness together. This is a lesson of acceptance which the turbulent events of the novel have taught them. Yet it is a truth, too, with a strong Buddhist resonance, for, to Buddhists, change is an inescapable fact of human existence from which no one is exempt. Paradoxically, the McKennas' unhappy brush with Buddhism has resulted in a married couple of whom Jimmy's Rinpoche would now be justly proud.

6. BUDDHISM IN *BUDDHA DA*

Buddha Da offers a rich reading experience, complete in itself, whether the reader has any knowledge of Buddhism or not. Some familiarity with the elements of Buddhism, however, helps reveal the full subtlety of Donovan's art. She herself has never been a practising Buddhist, but has in the past studied elements of Buddhism and attended meditation classes, appreciating their calming effect in daily life.

The introduction of an Eastern religion in the novel came about by chance. In an interview with the *Barcelona Review* Donovan explains:

> *Buddha Da* started with the voice of Anne Marie, talking about her da, and it wasn't till she came out with the bits about Jimmy becoming a Buddhist that I knew he was going to do this! [...] I hadn't been consciously thinking about meditation or Buddhism but here it was.

The attraction of Buddhist meditation was that it appeared to Donovan to be the most unlikely thing Jimmy could take up, given his previously extroverted, unreflecting attitude to life and, indeed, his indifference to religion generally.

On closer inspection, however, Jimmy McKenna's interest in Buddhism contributes more than simply a plot mechanism for the author. At one level, the novel explores a structural philosophy quite common in Western literature and popular culture: the idea that we do not fully appreciate the true value of our present situation until lived experience makes that value fully apparent. This idea turns up in many guises, in works as diverse as T.S. Eliot's poem *Little Gidding* or the film *The Wizard of Oz*.

Jimmy and Liz exemplify a variation on this idea: they are happy in their life together but, like many couples who have been together a long time, they are not always mindful of the riches they enjoy together. They explore independently aspects of their personalities, a departure which jeopardises not only their relationship with each other but with their daughter. The resulting pain brings belated recognition of the happiness they formerly enjoyed, but of which they had temporarily lost sight.

It is a measure of Anne Donovan's art, however, that she can combine an idea familiar in Western culture with elements of Buddhist philosophy to give her narrative an added resonance. An awareness of this layering, while not indispensable to enjoyment of the novel, enhances significantly the reading experience. Buddhist ideas permeate the text in various places, but not intrusively, and are sometimes placed in the mouths of minor characters or are found in acts performed by characters who have no knowledge or liking of Buddhism. For example, when Liz clears out her mother's house after the death of the old lady, she is carrying out a routine action for daughters in her position (pp.220–224). The act of clearing reminds Liz unpleasantly of her grudging attention to her mother in her latter days and brings her face to face with aspects of her personality of which she is somewhat ashamed. This act is very similar to the 'clearing' action the Rinpoche recommends to Jimmy (pp.81–82) as being necessary for his meditation process if he is to come to terms with his unsatisfactory relationships with members of his family. Liz and Jimmy both undertake a similar 'clearing' process and are confronted with painful aspects of themselves in so doing; one performs the clearing as a matter of domestic course, the other as a Buddhist inspired activity. Anne Donovan thus leaves the reader with twin perspectives on a single act.

The quest for 'clarity'. Our life experience tells us that single-mindedness is often necessary to reach goals, but carried to excess, may result in self-centredness harmful not only to those around us, but eventually to ourselves as well. This is what happens to Jimmy whose single-minded pursuit of 'clarity' temporarily destroys his happiness. Such failure has parallels in Buddhism: Siddartha Gautama, the prince who 2,500 years ago was to become the holy man we know today as the Buddha, decided at one point to rid himself of all physical distractions but realised after much pain that the path he had been following had led to nothing and was obliged to return to a more moderate path. Only after Jimmy abandons his preoccupation with the 'self' and the self's desires does he become aware of the riches he has always had but failed to appreciate. This brings him to the clarity he had so long desired. The idea that enlightenment is all around us if only we have eyes to see it had already been indicated to him but dismissed as 'daft' when mentioned by the 'French lama' that he had disliked so heartily (p.167). But Liz, no admirer of Buddhism, also considers (p.115) that clarity would come if only he opened his eyes to what was going on around him.

The effect of karma. Jimmy makes life choices which he does not properly think through. The result is his alienation from his wife and daughter. He behaves selfishly and as a result finds himself leading a lonely, unfulfilling existence. He discovers the hard way the Christian truth of 'whatsoever a man soweth, that shall he also reap' (Galatians Ch.6, V.7). But this is also an illustration of *karma,* the Buddhist law of cause and effect. Each action, even the smallest, will have its consequence either in this life or a later one. Jimmy causes pain to others by his own selfishness and is forced to suffer pain himself before acknowledging his error. Liz, too, in a rather different way, has to come uncomfortably to terms with the results of her actions in having an affair with a man who proves unsupportive when she is pregnant. Although she has always wanted another child, her pregnancy causes her much mental anguish. This is only resolved when she abandons the pride her mother accused her of and makes the first move in seeking Jimmy's help to broach the matter with Anne Marie.

Present, past and future. The Jimmy whom Anne Marie describes on page 1 is a larger-than-life, fun-loving figure, a fact which his behaviour at his brother's birthday party fully confirms. His decision, therefore, to cut himself off from much of what had made him the loveable, if wild, figure he is, cuts himself off from the very roots of his personality. Again, our life experience tells us that such radical breaks with our past may well be dangerous. On his Buddhist retreat, Jimmy had been told by a fellow student that 'truly being in the present encompasses both the past and the future', that they must all be 'held together as one'. In cutting himself off from the man he was, Jimmy, in Buddhist terms, is failing to 'encompass' his past into his present. His failure to acknowledge past errors and then simply move on more thoughtfully will have profound effects on both his present and future, as the novel explores. Towards the end of the novel (pp.314–315) we begin to see that Jimmy is beginning to appreciate how the destruction of other elements in his past, e.g. his old school, (which he had not even liked very much), brings him a real sense of loss and pain. Our past is part of who we are now, the novel suggests, and how we conduct our present shapes our future. And the future Jimmy has shaped for himself is a very different one from what he may have imagined. How he will 'encompass' it is left open by the author. The Jimmy we leave, however, is one who is much more fully present in the here-and-now than the Jimmy we first met, fully aware of his good fortune as husband and father.

7. FURTHER READING: *BEING EMILY*

In 2008, five years after the success of *Buddha Da,* Anne Donovan published her second novel, *Being Emily.* Here, too, her focus was on a close-knit Glasgow family, but seen this time, not from the multiple perspectives of the earlier novel, but rather from the viewpoint of a single narrator, Fiona O'Connell, whom we first meet as a second year pupil at a comprehensive school. The novel takes the form of what the Germans call a *bildungsroman,* a novel in which we watch the hero/heroine coming of age, frequently making many mistakes in the process. By the novel's end, Fiona is a married woman, expecting her first baby, installed once again in the flat in which the story begins. In the years in between, Fiona and her family suffer upsets which severely test their initial solidarity before an equilibrium is once again established. Again, the language of the novel is Glaswegian Scots.

Summary
The Catholic O'Connell family to whom we are introduced share a lively creativity. Fiona, a dreamy teenager much fixated on her heroine, Emily Brontë, the author of *Wuthering Heights,* sees herself initially as something of a poet before deciding to study art. Her elder brother, Patrick, is a baker with a penchant for painting fireplaces rather artistically; he later moves to London as a highly successful food stylist. Then there are the twins, Mona and Rona, who become Glasgow and West of Scotland line-dancing champions. Their West End flat, although somewhat overcrowded, is a bustling den of close-knit, good-humoured activity.

This comes abruptly to an end with the unexpected death of the mother in childbirth, Thereafter, the father falls apart, taking to drinking heavily while Fiona is left to cope, rather ineffectually, with the running of their home. In her misery, she welcomes the opportunity to move to a school in her sixth year where no one knows of the family tragedy. There she meets Jaswinder Singh, a Sikh fellow student, as much obsessed with Shelley as Fiona is with Emily Brontë. They become close. Mr O'Connell's drinking becomes worse and one night, in a drunken stupor, he accidentally sets fire to the house. He has failed to keep up payments on the insurance of the flat and the family finds itself homeless. Fiona's aunt, Janice, takes them in temporarily and, as a social worker, arranges a council flat to house them in. Fiona is furious at the loss of her beloved home and develops a hatred for her father. Such is her fury, she refuses initially to live under the same roof as him, and the novel sees her drifting, somewhat rootlessly, through a variety of temporary homes, nurturing a strong resentment towards the man who lost the home associated with her childhood and dead mother.

She finds some comfort in winning a prize for an art installation which persuades her to study at Glasgow College of Art after leaving school, while Jas decides, pragmatically, to study pharmacy at Aberdeen in order to enter the family firm. A refuge for her at this time is Jaswinder's home where she meets his musician brother, Amrik, to whom she is instantly attracted, abandoning Jas a day after she and Amrik become lovers. With Amrik she discovers physical passion in a way she had never explored with Jas and becomes pregnant before miscarrying. Amrik seems unmoved by all this and moves away to London, leaving Fiona physically and emotionally traumatised. A troubled period follows in which Fiona throws herself into her studies. The tragic pregnancy of her mother and her own miscarriage leave Fiona unhappily fixated with the idea of babies, which influences her work heavily. Her pain at losing the family home and her baby see Fiona drifting away from her sisters, which they attribute, perhaps correctly, to a certain snobbishness. Fiona's troubles are further exacerbated when she learns that Mona and her partner Declan are expecting what she wants most of all – a baby.

The birth of Grace is a turning point in the novel, for she fully lives up to her name, in that a kind of redeeming grace overtakes the unsettled O'Connells: frivolous Mona turns out to be an excellent mother, taciturn Declan turns out to be a tower of strength to Fiona in the technical aspects of her work, Mr O'Connell recovers his old self and Fiona herself, looking at Grace's 'smiley face', realises how awful she has been to others in her unhappiness. She feels ashamed at having sat in judgement on Mona and Declan and, seeking to start afresh, she goes finally to Confession, something she had avoided since the death of her mother. At Glasgow's Festival of Light she meets Jas again and gradually they resume their relationship. Fiona finally puts the burning down of their home behind her by working it into her art installation which, while it wins her academic success, inflicts great pain on her father, an incident which risks destabilising the newfound happiness among the O'Connells. It precipitates, however, a reconciliatory conversation between Fiona and her father, of the kind which they desperately needed to have had long before, but her father's shame and Fiona's anger have precluded it until now.

A more difficult conversation still needs to take place between Jas and Fiona when she tells him of her pregnancy with Amrik. A hurt Jas needs time to consider the implications this has for their relationship, but after reflection he proposes to Fiona after Mona and Declan's wedding, taking her to her old flat which he is acquiring. Fiona lives here on her own for three years until she and Jas finally marry. We leave a pregnant Fiona happily painting a mural whose content is far more serene than any of her artworks have been to date, fulfilled at last as an artist and woman.

The Brontë connection

Just as *Buddha Da* offered a complete reading experience without any knowledge of Buddhism, so, too, can *Being Emily* be enjoyed without detailed familiarity with Emily Brontë, her life and work. Nevertheless, some knowledge of the parallels between the lives of Fiona and Emily, and indeed of Emily's famous creation, Catherine Earnshaw, heroine of *Wuthering Heights,* adds a layer of interest and complexity to our experience of the novel.

Both Fiona and Emily are obliged to take over the running of the family home after the death of their mother (and aunt, in Emily's case); both lives are involved in artistic creativity; both have older brothers and two sisters (Emily had others who died); Fiona's mother dies in childbirth on the date (19th December) of Emily's death; both are reluctant to leave the surroundings of their upbringing; Fiona rescues her drunken father from a fire in the home in the same way that Emily rescued her drunken brother from a similar fire; like Cathy Earnshaw, Fiona mopes for the loss of her beloved family home; like Cathy, Fiona becomes involved passionately with a man who cannot bring her lasting happiness.

Before becoming too absorbed by these similarities, we should remember that for much of the time Anne Donovan draws a gentle humour, not from the parallels of the two lives, but from their contrasts: Fiona lives in the rough and tumble of twenty-first century tenement life in Glasgow, while Emily wandered the desolate moors of mid-nineteenth century Yorkshire. Donovan cleverly uses Fiona's Brontë fixation as a kind of metaphor for the young Fiona's over-romanticised view of the world. Ironically, were she to look at her own life as it is, she would see she is uncomfortably surrounded by events as colourful as any found in a Brontë novel: a mother dying in childbirth; the family home destroyed by fire; a daughter's brave rescue of a father from the conflagration; a friend's father killed by lightning; a passionate but ultimately unhappy affair with an exotically handsome sitar-playing Indian.

Gradually, Fiona commits herself to a more rational view of the world, one taught her by many painful life experiences, one no longer privileging the fancifully exotic over the more prosaic claims of reconciliation, family solidarity and emotional stability. She eventually learns a full appreciation of her late mother's wisdom and practicality. In the novel's closing pages she acknowledges that all she has to rely on is 'the spirit inside me, the one she'd [her mother] helped tae shape and form.' Yet, her new found realism does not extinguish her admiration for the now unfashionable 'ideal' by which characters lived their lives in the work of Emily Brontë and Shelley, an ideal which she still sees alive in Jas:

> I wanted to live my life by an ideal: nae compromises, nae conditions. And I couldnae imagine daeing that with anyone but Jas. (p. 269)

The role of creativity
The novel opens in a dance and ends with a mural. In between, we encounter a welter of different creative forms and talents. There is Fiona's talent in the visual arts (although poetry also beckoned at one point), Amrik's sitar-playing, Jas's photography, the twins' line-dancing, Patrick's food-styling talents and even Declan's carpentry. For most of the novel's characters, creativity helps define their characters, yet it does not enjoy the centrality in their lives which it does in the case of Fiona and Amrik.

The contrasting relationship of Fiona and Amrik to their respective arts occupies much of the novel's attention. For Amrik, life is a mere distraction from his music and he divorces his art from it entirely, drifting on when personal circumstances, such as Fiona's miscarriage, begin to interfere with his music-making. For Fiona, her art is her way of coming to terms with the raw material of her life. We find her at work in the course of the novel on three art installations. Two of them involve babies: the first the baby which she blames for the death of her mother; the second is inspired both by the baby she lost herself and the resentment she feels towards Mona's baby; the third installation focuses on the home she lost through her father's negligence. All three are her way of working through the pain and bitterness of biographical events. All three are angry creations, the output of a soul in torment. Only when peace descends on her own life can she create the more serene art in the baby's room, where we find her at the novel's conclusion.

The spiritual dimension
While the novel deals with Fiona's progress towards fulfilment both as woman and artist, Anne Donovan charts, too, Fiona's spiritual progress through the novel. Chapel-going was part of the O'Connells' routine when Fiona was a child. After the death of her mother, she is overtaken by hatred for the baby that she blames for taking her mother from them. Chapel-going and confession become more irregular for all the family and Fiona can only confess trivia to the priest, feeling unable to talk of the hatred she feels for the dead

baby. Finally, she stops going to confession altogether. With Easter imminent, Fiona is anxious to put matters right but a harsh sermon from a young priest convinces her of the futility of trying to confess to such an unsympathetic hearer. Hatred reappears in her life with the loss of the family home: this time it is aimed at her father. During this bitter period there also grows up in her a somewhat unChristian disdain for her line-dancing sisters. Fiona's emotional turmoil for much of the novel is paralleled by a bleak spiritual vacuum.

It is only with the birth of Grace, the daughter of Mona and Declan, that an important realisation comes to her:

> [...] looking at Grace's innocence, I realised how awful I'd been [...] I wanted to start over, be cleaned out. (p.200)

Grace's name is no coincidence. The Oxford English Dictionary defines 'grace' as 'the divine influence which operates in men to regenerate and inspire virtuous impulses'. From this realisation comes Fiona's impulse to make her first confession for three years and shortly afterwards she emerges from this long dark spiritual night into Glasgow's Festival of Light, an event which invited Glaswegians to view familiar landmarks, literally, in a new light (which is, of course, what Fiona is now beginning to do with familiar figures around her). Here she meets up with Jas again, thus launching a long period of personal and spiritual regeneration and reconciliation.

In her painting of a latter-day Virgin Mary hanging out washing in her back court helped by a young Jesus, we see on the final page of the novel the graphic celebration of Fiona's reaffirmation of her artistic, family and spiritual values.

The danger of assumptions

In an uneasy conversation with Patric, Fiona broaches the subject of the kiss between Patric and Amrik in front of Mr O'Connell:

> He never even knew you were gay.
>   Course he did.

> Did you ever tell him?
> Not in so many words but I assumed.
> Assumptions.
> Assumptions?
> Jas always used tae rant about them. It's assumptions that cause all the trouble. (p.221)

Throughout the novel various assumptions are made, largely due to the reluctance of various characters to discuss matters close to them: as well as Patric failing to discuss his sexuality with his father, Fiona and Jas in their early days together never quite articulate how matters stand between them; Fiona and her father do not discuss their feelings towards each other until long after the fire; Fiona never discusses with Patric the true nature of her relationship with Amrik, nor does she reveal to Jas until late in the novel the true nature of her relationship with his brother.

The result of these failures is that assumptions are made which may ultimately lead in many cases to misunderstandings and pain. If forgiveness and reconciliation are to be at all possible, these assumptions need to be challenged through long-delayed personal discussions, of the kind we see only in the latter pages of the novel. The establishment of the real state of affairs is itself not without pain, but Fiona is particularly conscious of the need to eradicate assumptions or else, as she puts it, these 'unspoken' lies behave like weeds, and weeds:

> [...] left too long [...] creep round healthy plants and destroy them. (p.258)

Being Emily is a quiet plea not just for tolerance and forgiveness, but, if the painful hazards of assumptions are to be avoided, for greater openness and frankness in human relationships.

SELECTED BIBLIOGRAPHY

Short Story Collection by Anne Donovan
Hieroglyphics and Other Stories: Canongate, Edinburgh, 2001.

Novels by Anne Donovan
Buddha Da: Canongate, Edinburgh, 2003
Being Emily: Canongate, Edinburgh, 2008

Criticism
Bissett, Alan: 'The "New Weegies": The Glasgow Novel in the Twenty-first Century', in B. Schoene (Ed.) *The Edinburgh Companion to Contemporary Scottish Literature* (pp.59–67). Edinburgh University Press, Edinburgh, 2007
Burgess, Moira: *Imagine a City: Glasgow in Literature*. Argyll Publishing, Glendaruel, Argyll, 1998
Gale, Patrick: 'A pint of Heavy and a Glass of Moselle', *The Daily Telegraph* (p.8), 8 March 2003
Goring, Rosemary: 'She's Talking Our Language Now', *The Herald* (p.14), 4 January 2003
Scott, Jeremy: 'Talking back at the Centre: Demotic Language in Contemporary Scottish Fiction', in *Literature Compass* 2 20C 148, (pp.1–26), 2005

Website Interview
www.barcelonareview.com/37/e_ad_int.htm (2003)